Y0-BDX-679

18-42

Gagaku Bugaku The Left Dance "Genjôraku"

JAPANESE LIFE AND CULTURE SERIES

TUGE Hideomi: *Historical Development of Science and Technology in Japan*

INOUE Mitsusada: *Introduction to Japanese History Before the Meiji Restoration*

WATANABE Shoko: *Japanese Buddhism, A Critical Appraisal*

USHIOMI Toshitaka: *Forestry and Mountain Village Communities in Japan, A Study of Human Relations*

KAWAZOE Noboru: *Contemporary Japanese Architecture*

NAKAMURA Mitsuo: *Modern Japanese Fiction 1868–1926*

KAIGO Tokiomi: *Japanese Education, Its Past and Present*

TAKAHASHI Masao: *Modern Japanese Economy Since 1868*

KISHIBE Shigeo: *The Traditional Music of Japan*

ISIDA Ryuziro: *Geography of Japan*

THE TRADITIONAL MUSIC OF JAPAN

By
KISHIBE Shigeo

KOKUSAI BUNKA SHINKOKAI
(Japan Cultural Society)
Tokyo, 1969

First edition, 1966
Revised edition, 1969

Published by KOKUSAI BUNKA SHINKOKAI, *1-1-18, Shirokanedai, Minato-ku, Tokyo, Japan. Distributed by* JAPAN PUBLICATIONS TRADING COMPANY, *I. P. O. Box No. 5030, Tokyo; 1255 Howard Street, San Francisco, California 94103; 175 Fifth Avenue, New York, New York 10010.*

Printed in Japan

LCC Card No. 73-75822

Publisher's Foreword

It has long been regretted that students and scholars who engage in Japanese studies have to face many difficulties, not only in having to master a difficult language, but also in the matter of the lack of effective assistance by the learned institutions and people of this country. Recognizing this fact, the Kokusai Bunka Shinkokai (Japan Cultural Society), since shortly after its establishment in 1934, has been applying its energies to several programs for providing such facilities for foreign students and friends of Japan.

Initially the Society made a collection of Western-language books and magazines relating to Japan, which are available for reference at the K.B.S. Library, and published a full catalogue of the items collected during the years 1935–62, *A Classified List of Books in Western Languages Relating to Japan,* which is obtainable from the University of Tokyo Press.

Concurrently, since 1959 the Society has been compiling a series of bibliographies, under the series title *A Bibliography of Standard Reference Books for Japanese Studies with Descriptive Notes,* listing and describing the more important books written on Japan in Japanese. This is proving another valuable contribution to Japanese studies. Volumes already published cover the following fields: Generalia, Geography and Travel, History and Biography, Religion, History of Thought, Education, Language, Literature, Arts and Crafts, Theatre-Dance-Music, Manners and Customs and Folklore, Economy. In preparation are volumes on: Politics, and Law.

Since 1961 the Society has also been publishing a series of books on Japanese life and culture, including the present publication, which give basic guidance in introductory fields of Japanese studies. Out of more than fifteen such published studies, the Society has now selected a number, as listed on the first page of this volume, which have been revised and reissued. More volumes, both revised and original editions, will appear successively. It is the sincere hope of the Society that this series, as well as its other activities, may prove of value to all who are interested in the study of Japan.

The author of the present volume, KISHIBE Shigeo, professor of the University of Tokyo, is one of the leading musicologists in Japan, making comparative studies of Japanese and other Asian music. His study in the eighth century Chinese music of the T'ang dynasty brought new light to the historiography of Asian music.

Our acknowledgement is due to the author for the compilation of the manuscript and for the selection of charts, maps, figures and photographs; and to the Music Department of the Imperial Household, the Tsubouchi Memorial Theatre Museum of Waseda University, the Young Buddhist Association of the Buzan school of Shingon sect, Messrs. MISUMI Haruo, HAGA Hideo and KIMURA Tadashi for preparing the photographs.

March, 1969

KOKUSAI BUNKA SHINKOKAI

Preface

Visitors to Japan will undoubtedly be surprised by the fact that the musical life of contemporary Japan is quite westernized by the abundance of classical European music as well as popular American and Latin music. This is, of course, one of the facets of the modernization of Japan since the Meiji Restoration of 1868. In Tokyo, five professional symphony orchestras present monthly concerts of Bach, Beethoven, Hindemith and other occidental composers. The musical fare of Japanese TV is dominated by American jazz and popular songs, or music and dance by Japanese, but in the American style. At schools, Western songs are taught by teachers who are trained only in Western music. The traditional music appears to have been forgotten.

This is true to some extent. However, as the life of present-day Japan in general shows a kind of mixture of Eastern tradition and Western civilization, traditional music has not been preserved as merely a traditional curiosity. It is still very much a part of the everyday life of the modern Japanese in their almost inborn feelings of rhythm and melody.

March 1966

Shigeo Kishibe

Contents

Editorial Notes

1. Names of Japanese persons are written in Japanese style, namely family name first, followed by the first name.
2. Records corresponding to the explanations in this book may be obtained from Victor Company of Japan, Ltd., under the same title (or Victor, JL-32~4)

List of Plates

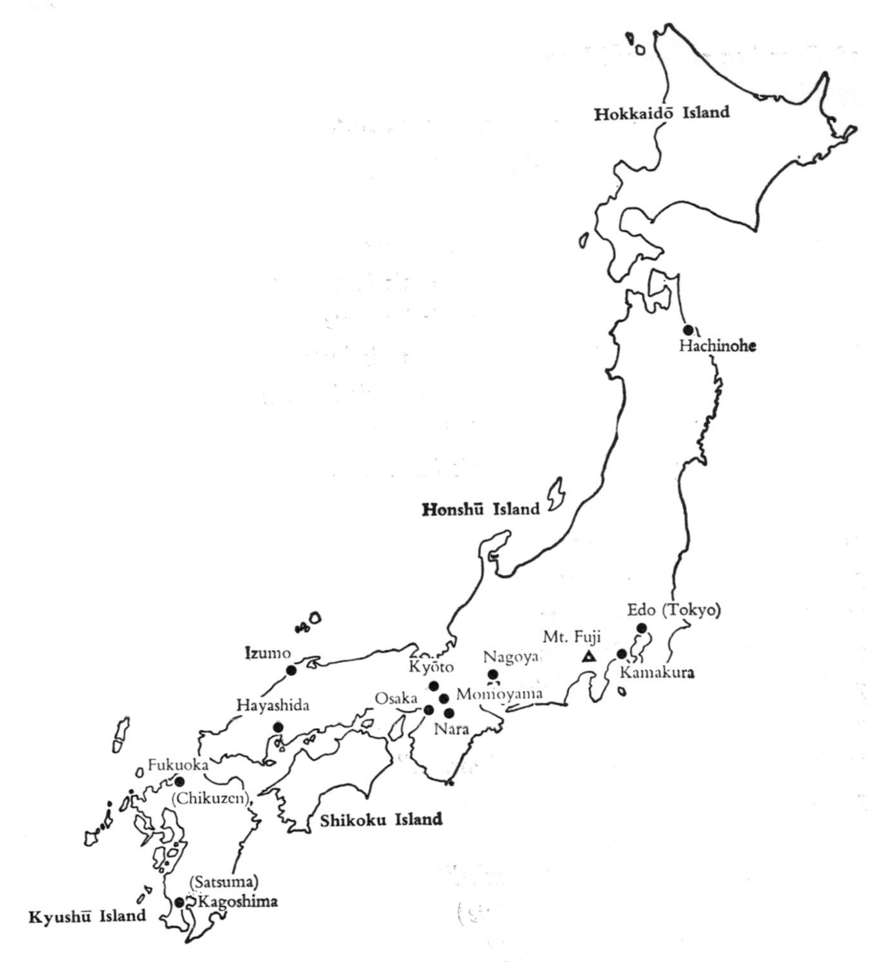

Fig. 1 Map of Japan

CHAPTER I

History

The history of Japanese traditional musical style can be conveniently divided into five periods. These correspond to the five major periods of social, political and economic development as shown in Chart 1.

Ancient times, with a system of clans and slave labour, can be split into two periods, the early and later. The early primitive clan-slave labour system developed and was formalized in course of time by a series of the governments. The country became a cultured nation partly through the introduction of the Chinese arts of the T'ang dynasty.

	Music	Date and names of political period	Society
1. Early Ancient	Period of Native Music	—— 6th century	Society of primitive clan-system
2. Later Ancient	P. of International M.	Asuka, Nara, Early Heian (7—10th c.)	Society of clan-system organized under governmental control
3. Early Middle Ages	P. of National M. (1)	Later Heian, Kamakura, Muromachi (11—16th c.)	Feudal society
4. Later Middle Ages	P. of National M (2)	Momoyama, Edo (17th c.—1868)	Feudal society dominated by Tokugawa Shogunate
5. Modern Times	P. of World M.	Meiji era—— (1868——)	Society of Industrial Capitalism and Socialism

Chart 1. Chronological divisions in styles of Japanese traditional music

Asuka (592–628 A.D.) is the period of the introduction of Chinese Buddhism. It was at this time that the Hôryûji Temple, the world's oldest extant wooden building, was constructed. The Nara period (710–793), the name of which originates from the name of the city (see Fig. 1) where the capital was located, is well remembered as the time when the country was most active in the enthusiastic absorption of the culture of China, including music. In this period also the Great Buddha, the colossal bronze statue of Tôdaiji, was erected upon the order of the Emperor Shômu. In the Heian period which followed (794–1191), the capital shifted to Kyôto, which remained the capital of Japan until 1868. In the early half of this period, Japanese culture was supported by aristocrat and bureaucrat alike.

In the later Heian period, the Samurai (feudal warrior) began to exert a great influence in cultural circles. About the same time the Genji family established the first feudal government (Shogunate) of Kamakura (1192–1337). This was followed by the Muromachi period (1338–1573) in which the Ashikaga family established a Shogunate. Both period names stem from those of the capitals of the epochs: Kamakura, from the city, 30 miles south-west of Tokyo and Muromachi, from the name of the area in the city of Kyôto, where the Shogunates were located. Cultural activities in the first half of the Middle Ages found their focus in the lives of the Samurai clans and the Buddhist priests.

The Muromachi period was followed by the Momoyama period (1574–1602) and then the Edo period (1603–1867). It was in the Edo period that the Shogunate truly dominated the nation.

A spirit of nationalism began to supplant the intercultural trend of the former periods. The increasing activity of merchants whose society created its own new culture of special interest. This was one of the leading cultural stimuli during the Tokugawa Shogunate, or Edo period, which lasted for 265 years.

Since the Meiji Restoration of 1868, which coincided with the opening of Japan to the outside worlds, a period of sudden modernization came about through the introduction of new industrial methods and ideas of civilization from the West. This was coupled, at least theoretically, with the return of the Emperor to the exercise of governmental power. Emperors had lived a rather passive existence since the Kamakura period. With the Meiji Restoration much of Japanese traditional culture became, at least temporarily, displaced as a result of the widespread interest in things Western. And again, since the Second World War, another wave of intensive internationalism, often inspired by socialism, has, to some extent, wrought changes in Japanese society and culture. This fifth period may be termed the period of "World Culture".

The historical changes in the styles of Japanese music correspond to the previously mentioned periods of social and cultural history. The early ancient period displayed primitive and aboriginal music, the features of which are only vaguely known. This was followed by the later ancient period, when music from the Asian Continent, first Korea and then China, created epoch-making changes in Japanese music (see Chart 2). Chinese music of the T'ang dynasty had felt the influence of music from India, Iran and Central Asia. This means Japan was included in the circle of Far Eastern intercultural music. Fig. 2 shows an example of the eastward stream of music from West and South Asia, specifically informative as to how three kinds of lute were introduced to Japan.

The lutes of the three types, which were used in a great concert held at Tôdaiji Temple in 752 for the celebration upon the completion of the Great Buddha, have been preserved in the Imperial Treasury of Shôsôin at Nara. The four-stringed lute (Biwa) has its predecessor in the ancient Iranian four-stringed lute (Barbat). It had journeyed eastward through Gandhâra (Afghanistan), Khotan (Chinese Turkistan) and China, where it was called Bi-ba, or P'i-p'a in present day Chinese.

The five-stringed lute (Gogenbiwa) finds its roots in ancient India and was introduced to China by another route through Central Asia. The Wu-hsien-p'i-p'a in today's Chinese corresponds to Gogenbiwa, using the same Chinese characters. This lute followed a course to South East Asia (Burma, Java and Cambodia), but did not find its way to China through the Chinese Sea from South East Asia, as might be expected. The third lute having a round body was a native Chinese instrument called Yüan-hsien or Genkan in Japanese pronounciation, again employing the

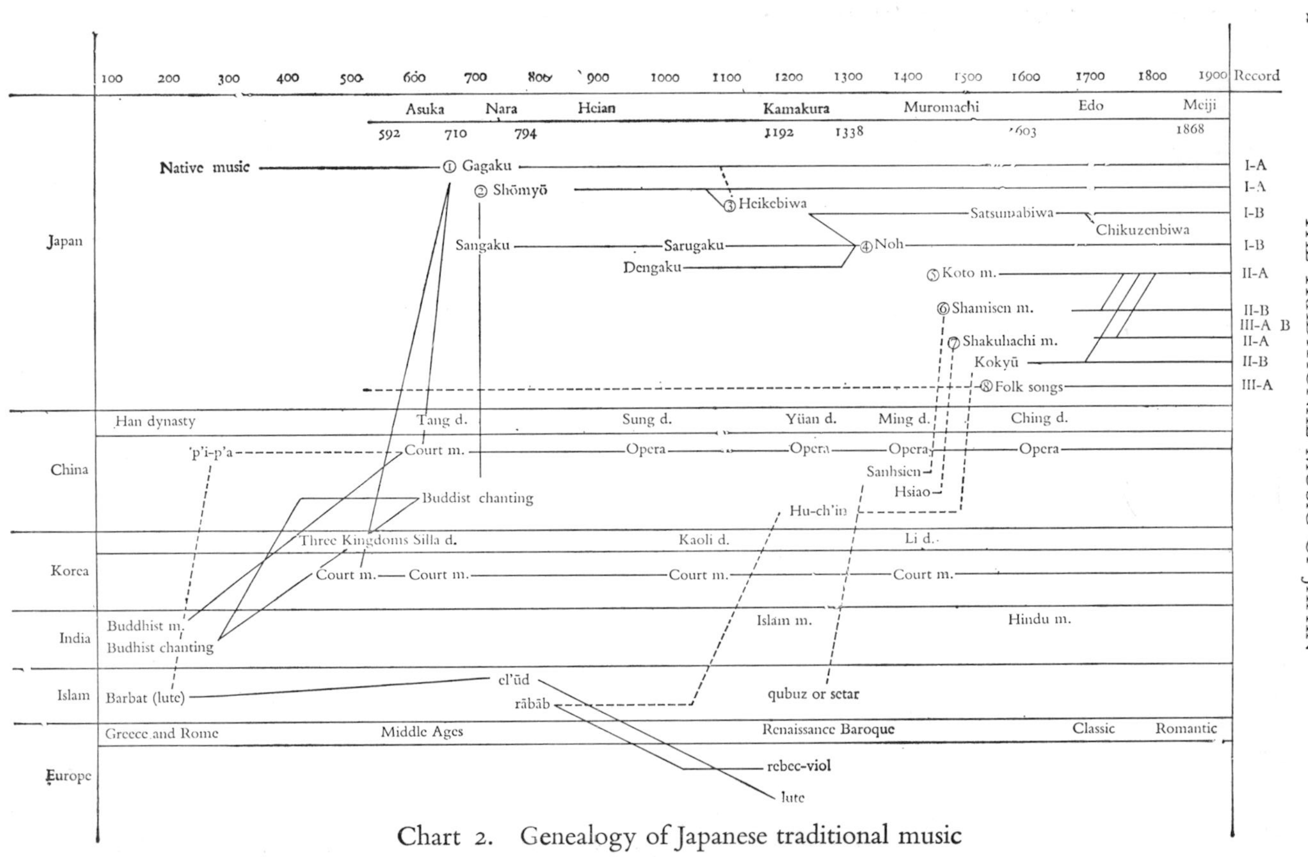

Chart 2. Genealogy of Japanese traditional music

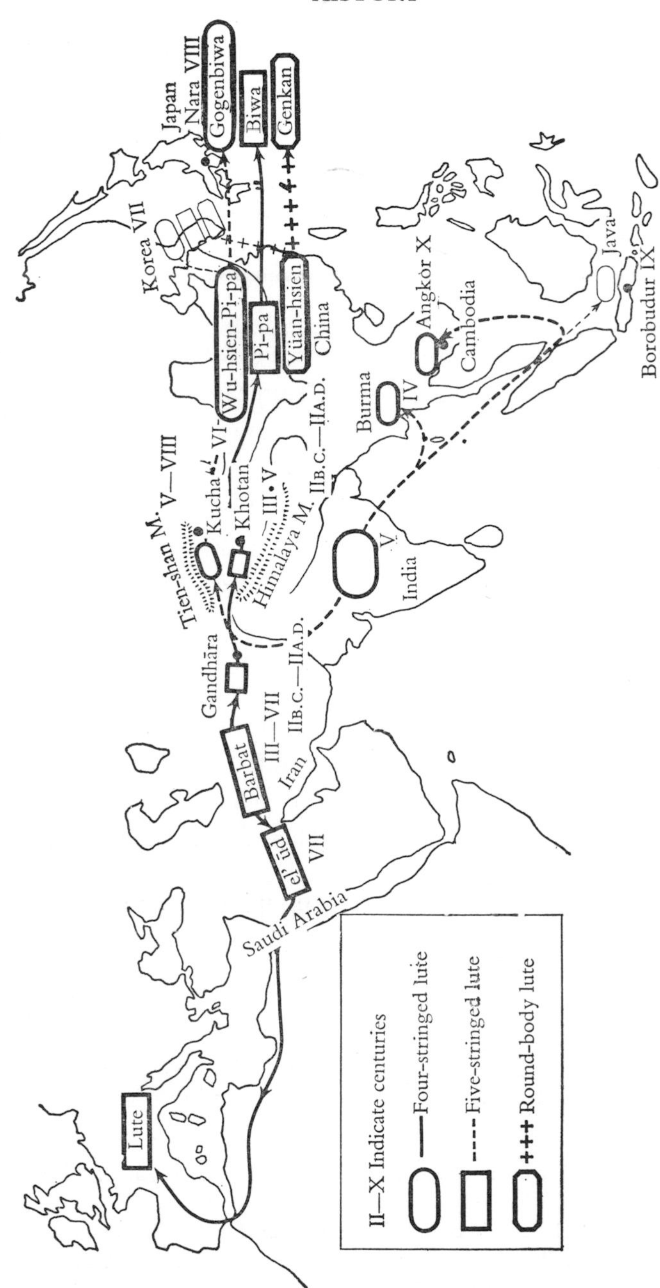

Fig. 2 Map indicating the eastward stream of music from west and south Asia

same Chinese characters. Another interesting fact is that the Iranian Barbat later became the Arabian "El'ûd" which is the precursor of the European "lute", in design as well as in the name of the instrument.*

The representative music of this period was "Gagaku" (see Chart 2), court music consisting of Chinese, Korean, Indian and native music. "Shômyô" (Buddhist chanting) which had its beginning in India was introduced through China, and formed another major variety of music. While both Gagaku and Shômyô were modified to suit Japanese taste, they kept their original style to a remarkable extent, and two new major kinds of music of quite a national nature appeared in the early Middle Ages. These were Heikebiwa in the Kamakura period, and Noh in the Muromachi period. Heikebiwa was new and unique, and was to be the origin of narrative music. This is one of the most important and specific styles of Japanese music. The accompanying instrument, the Biwa, a short lute, was an adaptation of the Gagaku Biwa. The Heikebiwa was later followed by not only the Satsumabiwa and Chikuzenbiwa, but also by some Shamisen music. This Shamisen music is particularly evident in Gidayû which is the most accomplished style of narrative music.

Another form of narrative music is that of the Noh. In this form the narrative is accompanied by flute and drums together with theatrial performance. Noh represents the perfect marriage of literature, theatre, music and dance. It also represents the highest degree of Japanese aesthetics in the arts.

Contrary to the music of the early Middle Ages which was largely sponsored by the Samurai and the Buddhist priests, who were the high classes of society, the three new major genres of music occurred among merchants and artisans in the cities of the latter Middle Ages of Momoyama and Tokugawa periods. They constituted the lower class of the feudal society together with peasants. This music consisted of Koto, Shamisen and Shakuhachi. The Koto (a long zither-like instrument with thirteen silk strings) was adapted from the Koto of Gagaku. The Koto is

* Shigeo Kishibe: "The Origin of the P'i-p'a (Chinese Lute) with Particular Reference to Three Kinds of Lute Preserved in the Imperial Treasury of Shôsôin". Proceedings of Asiatic Society of Japan, New Series XIX, 1940.

unique in that it was the first instrument for accompanying song as well as a solo instrument in its own right.

The Shamisen (three-stringed banjo-like, long necked lute) originates in the Chinese San-hsien. The instrument used only as an accompanying instrument gained great favour in Japan. It produced many schools of music through skillful performance techniques and slight and delicate variations. These schools of Shamisen music include those of narrative music coming from the previously mentioned Biwa-narrative music, as well as those of lyrical singing. The schools of Shamisen music are explained in detail in the next chapter.

The Shakuhachi (end blown or vertical bamboo flute) has its beginning in the Chinese vertical flute (Hsiao). It first appeared in the Muromachi period being much shorter (one foot and one inch) and called the "Hitoyogiri". In the Edo period, the present length of the Shakuhachi (one foot and eight inches) was used by itinerant Buddhist priests. Then in the Middle Edo period, the music was modified into solo art music. It was at the close of the Edo period that the instrument began to join the ensemble of Koto and Shamisen establishing the ensemble style of music called "Sankyoku" (literally meaning three instruments).

Another instrument which must be mentioned is the Kokyû (three or four-stringed bowed lute). This is the only bowed lute of Japan, and its use was rare. Once again its origins were Chinese, and it was used in the ensemble of Koto and Shamisen. Later, however, the Shakuhachi took the place of the Kokyû in the ensemble, and the Kokyû fell into disuse. For this reason, the music of this instrument is not regarded as one of the major genres of the period.

In the later Middle Ages of Edo, the three major genres of music (Shamisen, Koto, and Shakuhachi) were held in great esteem, while the older music of Gagaku, Biwa, and Noh was also still in favour. However, following the Meiji Restoration of 1868, the traditional music began its decline. Since then, and for a hundred years, Japan has been enthusiastic over Western music, both classical and popular. Although traditional music gradually lost some of its importance, the previously mentioned major genres of traditional music still survive today in the minds of the people. In addition, folk songs and folk music are very much alive in present day Japan. Though folk music originated in early and obscure times, the history of most of the existing folk music can be traced to the beginning of the Edo period and later.

For the readers' information, Chart 2 shows a chronological comparison between the music of the East and West. The reader will discover not only how each period of the history of Japanese music corresponds to the periods of the history of Western music, but will also find important and basic differences regarding fixed dates in the development of music and society. Simply stated, the end of the later Ancient Period in Japan occurred five hundred years later than that of Europe (Greece and Rome). The Middle Ages in Japan, therefore, came about five hundred years later than in Europe. This period lasted for one thousand years, while that of Europe lasted for eight hundred years; and the Modern Age in Japan commences with the second half of the 19th century, while that of Europe begins with the 15th century if one accepts the hypothesis that Baroque polyphony is the start of Modern music.

It should be pointed out here that the author has tried to describe only historical facts in the preceding paragraphs rather than attempting an estimated evaluation of music by comparing East and West. It is extremely difficult to evaluate the various kinds of the world's music because of the differences in style, aesthetics, and background. What the author intends to impart to the reader who is going to listen, perhaps for the first time, to foreign music, is some general preparation and some insight into the relationships, the similarities, the differences in the world's varied musics. It is also to be pointed out that modern Western music is not the only music which has reached the hearts and soul of man. It cannot be too emphatically stated that there are many musical ideas which have not been attempted in Western music, but have found their way into non-Western music.

CHAPTER II

Characteristics

(a) Characteristics, historically considered

Traditional music varies not only according to historical conditions as mentioned, but also according to social and geographical conditions. One of the most interesting facts about the study of the history of Japanese music is that almost all of the major musics which originated in the Ancient (8th century), the Middle (9th–18th centuries) and the rather recent period (19th century) have been preserved without great alteration. Gagaku has its source in the 8th century. The Noh was established in the 15th century, and Shamisen was in full bloom in the 17th–19th centuries. Chikuzenbiwa music appeared in the latter half of the 19th century, when Western music began to make its influence felt in Japan. The music of this instrument is usually in the pure traditional style.

The styles of music largely depended upon the varing historical changes in society. Gagaku was supported by the ancient court, government and aristocracy, while Noh was under the sponsorship of the feudal lords. Shamisen music developed in the society of the merchant in the latter half of the feudal period in Japan (the 17th century through the early half of the 19th century).

An interesting social note may be found in the music of the Biwa and Koto. These instruments were played by blind persons who were protected by the Government in a specific social system which was called *Shokuyashiki* (House of Profession). The Shintô shrines and Buddhist temples were after a fashion patrons of music (Gagaku, Noh, Shakuhachi) and musicians of Heikebiwa and Shakuhachi formerly were Buddhist) priests. Shômyô (Buddhist chanting) was used for Buddhist ceremonies.

Another item of interest from the social standpoint is the fact that societies of musicians have been fairly conservative in maintaining their old organizational structure for self-preservation. Musicians made up groups, sects and schools. The chief of each school, called "Iemoto" has been succeeded by sons or students without an interruption. The chief controls, not only the political and economic conditions of the society, but even the style of the art.

A student who established a new style would be expelled from the school in spite of economic and social risk. For over 350 years, for example, no one has been able to establish a new school of Noh other than the five existing schools. In contrast to this is Shamisen music which, being more popular, was permitted the establishment of quite a number of schools and sects.

Since the Heian period (the 9th–12th centuries), Japan has had two major cultural centres, Kyôto and Edo (present-day Tokyo). Kyôto where the capital had been located for over one thousand years (following 794 A.D.) was the centre of older culture. Osaka only a few miles southwest of Kyôto became another important city, through its economic development in the Edo period (1603–1867).

The area comprising Kyôto and Osaka, was called Kamigata (upper place) in contrast to Edo where the Tokugawa Shogunate (principal feudal lord) was established. The Shogunate was actually the political power of Japan. In Edo as well as Osaka, the activity of the merchant, both in economics and culture, established a new style of music, that is Shamisen music. This music is most commonly linked with the Kabuki theatre, and the puppet theatre (Bunraku). It is necessary to note that in regard to style and mood, there has been a big difference between Edo and Kamigata, especially in the field of Shamisen and Koto music. Even today, the Kamigata mood controls the area west to Kyôto while the Edo mood dominates the area east to Tokyo.

Religions, especially Buddhism, had an influence, not only in the textual content of songs and drama, but in the area of musical aesthetics. With the idea of Jôdo (Paradise) and resignation of the present life, Buddhist ideas began, in the Kamakura period to dominate the themes of Heikebiwa and Noh. In the Edo period, the idea of the lovers' suicide often appeared in dramas and songs of unhappy love. Zen Buddhism had its special influence through the introduction of rigid discipline into the methods of teaching and studying music, which resulted in a high degree of refinement and formalization.

Confucianism, especially through the ideals of loyalty and filial piety, became the most important moral stimuli, not only in themes and texts, but also in the purpose of its creation. In the music of the feudal period Confucianism acted as an ethical principle in teaching and learning. The tight relationship between the chief and the members of the school was further supported by this morality.

Shintoism had its influence not only through ceremonial music, but also through one of the basic idea of Shintoism, that musical art is given by the gods. This attitude dominated the aesthetics of music, even of the Edo period. Often the miracle of music was commented upon from this point of view, rather than from any more logical theory.

(b) Characteristics, technically considered

Japanese traditional music varies a great deal as is now evident and its musical characteristics cannot be easily described in a simple manner. However, the following points may be said to be its principal characteristics:

1. Monophonic Nature

Except for the instrumental ensemble of Gagaku, Japanese traditional music attempts to reach the highest beauties of monophonic music. Polyphony did not develop to the extent that it did in Western music. Instead of the harmonic feature, Japanese music became involved in minute tones, free rhythm, and delicate timbre, of an order higher than that achieved in Western music.

2. Tone System

Two types of five-tone modes (Notation 1) are most often used for Koto, Shamisen, and folk music, while the seven-tone system is the basis for Gagaku (Notation 7); and the specific tone system of Noh is based upon the tetrachord (Notation 2). These modes or tonalities are based upon a twelve-tone system, which is slightly different from the modern equal-tempered chromatic scale, since it is arranged by compiling the pure fourth and fifth alternately. This is the same as compiling the fifth in the Pythagorean scale.

Fig. 3 Notation 1

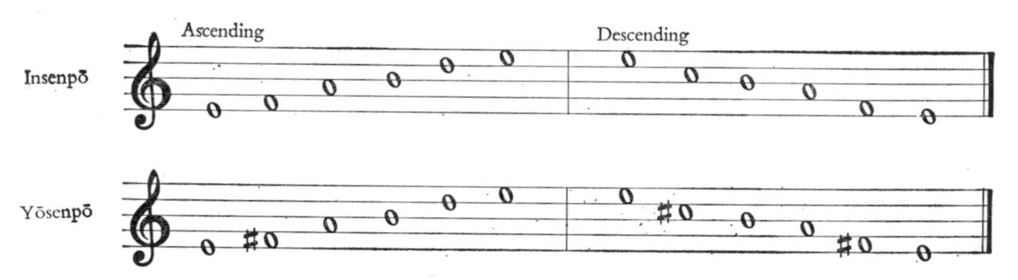

3. Melodic Pattern

Melodic composition is often based upon the idea of arrangement of melodic patterns. Representative examples are found in the singing of Noh and Gidayû.

4. Free Rhythm

Beside the mechanical fitted rhythm, which is usual in Western music after the Middle Ages, free rhythm, which cannot be reduced to a measurement of an equal number of beats, figures importantly in Japanese music. This is particularly apparent in the music of the Noh, in which we may find the highest degree of refinement regarding free rhythm.

5. Timbre

While in Western music a wide range of variety of timbre (bowed string, wood-wind, brass instruments) exists, in Japanese traditional music there is a rather narrower range of variety of timbre (plucked string, bamboo wind instruments). However, the variety of timbre between Japanese instruments of the same type shows more delicacy than in western instruments. For example, there are more than ten kinds of Shamisen having only slight differences according to the style of the music. It is of importance for both performance and for appreciation to be able to distinguish the delicate difference. This delicacy of timbre is also derived from the fact that noise is combined with musical sound as an important element of timbre. The employment of noise has its base in the natural sounds held in special favour bv the Japanese.

6. Synthetic Nature

As to aesthetics, one of the basic features is the fact that the majority of the music is vocal and has been created in combination with literature, theatre and dancing. "Absolute music" of a purely instrumental ensemble can be found only in Gagaku, Koto, Shakuhachi and folk music. Noh is the most representative genre of this kind of synthesis in stage art.

Beauty through stylish and sober refinement has been a basic element of Japanese taste since the Middle Ages. There is an avoidance of overly brilliant, superficial beauty. The aesthetical terms of "Yûgen" in Noh and "Iki" in Shamisen music are based on this idea. As a result spirit is more appreciated than technique.

Finally, the position of Japanese traditional music in the music of Asia should be discussed briefly. As the natural result of geographical circumstances, the Japanese Islands are located at an extreme point, set apart from the continent. Therefore, the music of Japan has had long periods in which to develop independently. However the waves of cultural influence from the continent have also remarkably stimulated Japanese music.

This is specially so in the later half of the Ancient period, the Nara and Heian periods. Even in the Middle Ages when nationalism dominated, instruments (Shamisen, Shakuhachi, etc.) were introduced from China. But the Shamisen, for example, was modified to a great extent and the music for the instrument is quite different from the Chinese music for the San-hsien, the forerunner of Shamisen.

In spite of this independent use of imported musical instruments, the general features of Japanese traditional music impress us with the ways in which it has preserved many of the elements of music from the continent.

In addition to this historical relationship, there are characteristics common to the music of Japan and other nations of Asia, when compared to modern European music. For example: monophony (monomelodic line); delicate intonation of tone-system; free rhythm; emphasis upon timbre; connection to life, nature, theatrical and dancing; religious and ethical ideas, etc. However, before being drawn to the vast differences between East and West, one must realize that there are such differences between nations that it is difficult even for one Asian nation to understand the music of other nations of Asia.

One should also keep in mind that even the term modern western music may be used to refer to music, say, from only the 16th century, forgetting that there were many earlier styles of European music, some of which had elements in common with some Asian music.

The religious element in Japanese traditional music is much less than that of the music of India. For the Japanese taste, the music of China, Korea, Indonesia and India is too brilliant and colourful. One octave is divided into 22 tones in (ancient) India; into 17 tones in Arabia; into 7 tones in Thailand and into 5 tones in Indonesia. While in Japan and China, the twelve unequal-tempered system was used. Melodies are based upon these different tone systems, as well as the different 5 or 7 tone scales or modes which sound quite different from one another.

String instruments of India use metal strings, the timbre of which is much less appreciated than the silk string in Japan.

CHAPTER III

Outline of Eight Major Genres

(1) Gagaku (Court Music)

Gagaku, literally meaning elegant music, is the oldest surviving music in Japan. It was established in the court around 1200 years ago, and has been preserved at the Imperial Court and in some shrines and temples. Gagaku repertory today consists of the following four categories:

a) Instrumental ensemble (Kangen)
b) Dance music (Bugaku)
c) Songs
d) Ritual music for Shintô ceremonies.

Gagaku in its present form represents the system which was established in the early Heian period (the early half of the 9th century). This is a modification of the Gagaku of the Nara period, which was almost an exact imitation of the contemporary music of China and Korea.

Kangen, literally wind-and-string instruments, is an orchestral music and Bugaku (dance music) is an instrumental ensemble accompanying the dance. But for both, the instrumentation differs only slightly, thus they belong to one class, while the remaining two are vocal.

That last category, Shintô ritual music, differs from the others in that it is performed only for religious purposes, while the other three are employed at court ceremonies and banquets. It should be pointed out that the element of entertainment, very much alive in the ancient times, is today non-existent.

(a) Kangen and (b) Bugaku (Photos 1 and 2)

In the Nara period (7th century) over thirty kinds of instruments were used to perform music of China, Korea, India and the native music of Japan. The Department of Music of the Government and certain temples and shrines were in charge of this music.

In the previously mentioned Imperial Treasury of Shôsôin, seventeen kinds of instruments of the year 752 A.D. have been preserved. Among them, one finds several instruments which are not used by the present-day Gagaku: angular harp, five-stringed lute, round-bodied lute, 25 stringed, long zither, 12 stringed long zither, 7 stringed, long zither, vertical bamboo flute, pan-pipe, gong-chime, and various drums.

The present Kangen, as well as Bugaku, is classified into two groups, Sahô (left) and Uhô (right). Sahô music consists mainly of the music from China and several pieces originating in India while Uhô music

Chart 3 Kangen and Bugaku instruments

	Kangen	Bugaku
Sahô (Left)	Ryûteki (flute) Hichiriki (oboe) Shô (mouthorgan) Sô (zither) Biwa (lute) Kakko (side drum) Shôko (gong) Taiko (big drum)	Ryûteki Hichiriki Shô Kakko Shôko Taiko
Uhô (Right)	Komabue (flute) Hichiriki San no tsuzumi (side drum) Shôko Taiko	Komabue Hichiriki San no tsuzumi Shôko Taiko

consists mainly of the music from Korea and a few pieces from Manchuria. This classification seems to represent the combination of the ancient idea in Japan that left is superior to right, and the fact that in Japan at that time, Chinese music was more flourishing than Korean music. Many pieces composed in Japan were also classified in either left or right style. (Photos 22, 23, 24 & 25)

The instrumentation for Kangen as well as Bugaku is as shown in Chart 3. The Sô and Biwa are used only in the Left Kangen. The flute and side drum differ between Left and Right. The Shô is not used in the Right. The basic features and characteristics of these instruments and the way in which they are performed are as follows:

(i) Wind Instruments:

Ryûteki: (Photos 7 & 8) A transverse bamboo flute with seven finger holes, sounding d (closed), $d^\sharp$, e, $f^\sharp$, g, a, b, and d'.

Fig. 4 Hichiriki

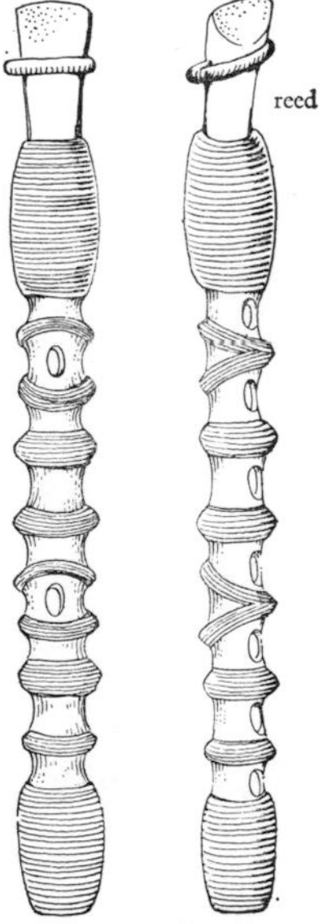

Komabue: A thinner and shorter transverse bamboo flute with six finger holes, producing higher notes, d♯ (closed), f♯, g, a, b, c♯ and e'. (Photo 8)
Hichiriki (Figure 4): A tiny oboe, the pipe of which is bamboo, having nine finger holes, seven on the front and two on the back. A thick double reed is inserted into the top of the pipe. The range of notes is g–a'. By controlling the reed the notes can be raised or lowered by a half tone or less. (Photos 5 & 6)

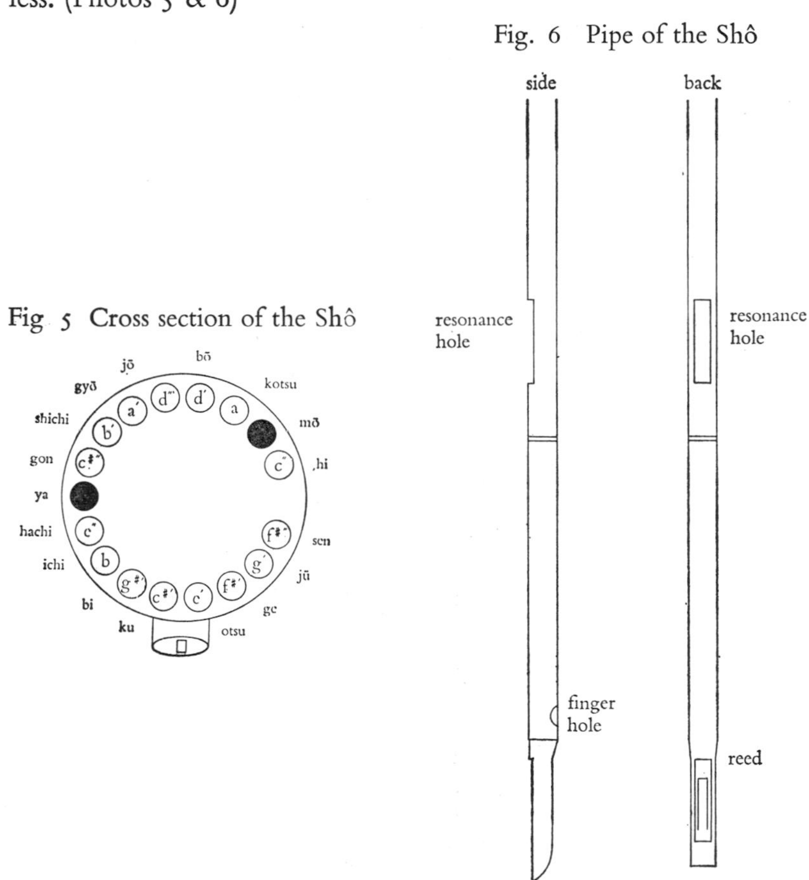

Fig. 6 Pipe of the Shô

Fig. 5 Cross section of the Shô

Shô (Photos 3 & 4): "Mouth Organ" consisting of a wooden windchest which is covered with a plate, made of water buffalo horn. Seventeen thin bamboo pipes are inserted through the cover. At the lower end of each pipe a metal reed, like a harmonica reed, is fixed except in two pipes which are mute (Figure 5). The instrument is blown through the mouthpiece fixed to the windchest. The sound of the reed is so tiny and high that it can scarcely be heard. Therefore, on the upper inside of each pipe, a thin, short slit is made which is approximately one inch in length (Figure 6). The air column in the part of the pipe between the closed bottom of the pipe and the lower end of the slit, resonates with the vibration of the reed, and makes the sound of the reed loud enough to be audible.

Since the instrument produces a harmony of five or six notes, the performer has to sound the correct pipes. Close to the cover, each pipe has a tiny finger hole. When the finger hole is open resonance does not occur, but when closed there is resonance and the pipe sounds.

The fingering technique on the instrument is not necessarily difficult because the order of pipes is not arranged in chromatic fashion, but is arranged in such a way that is convenient to produce the eleven given chords. This is shown below. (Notation 2)

The structure of these chords has not been solved definitely. They give off a Debussy-like quality. There are several points to be noted. First of all, chords include the discord of a' and b', and secondly, each seems to be based upon the circle of the fifths or fourths which comprises the ancient Chinese theory of twelve tones.

Fig. 7 Notation 2

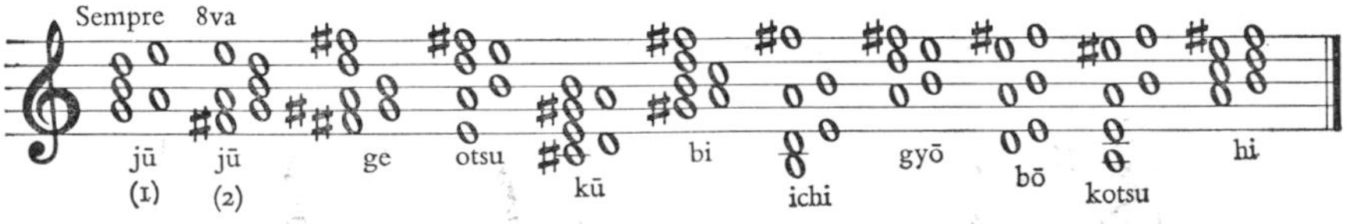

(ii) String Instruments:

The *Biwa* (Photo 9) is a four-stringed lute with a flat back side. The silk strings are used and are tuned in five ways according to tonality. (Notation 3) The strings are plucked with a wooden plectrum in arpeggio fashion, producing chords instead of melody. (Photo 10)

Fig. 8 Notation 3

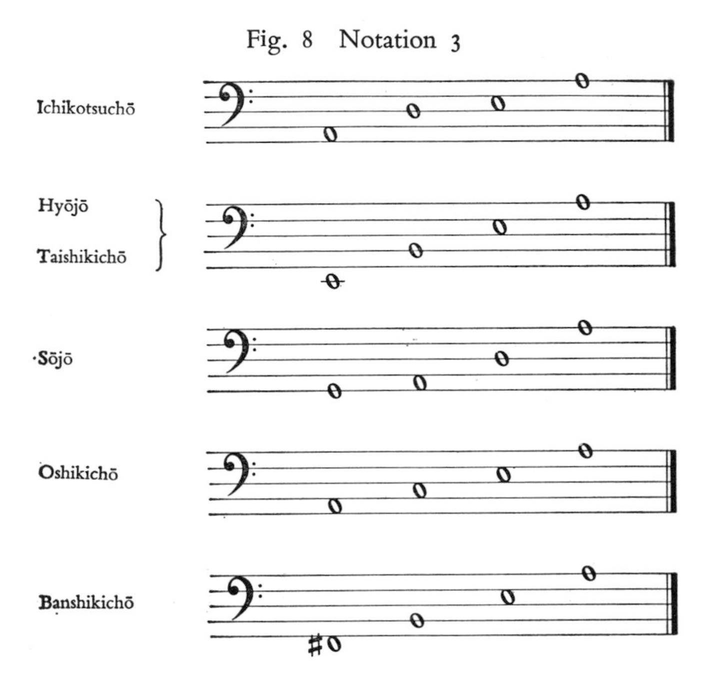

Sô, *Gakusô* or *Koto* (Photo 12): A thirteen-stringed long zither, some six feet in length, with silk strings, tuned by thirteen wooden bridges in six ways, as shown below, according to tonality used. The strings are plucked with three picks, which are made of bamboo and fixed to the thumb and two fingers of the right hand by leather bands (Notation 4).

Fig. 9 Notation 4

The instrument produces chords coinciding with the specific style of melodic patterns or arpeggios as shown in Notation 5 (Photo 12).

Fig. 10 Notation 5

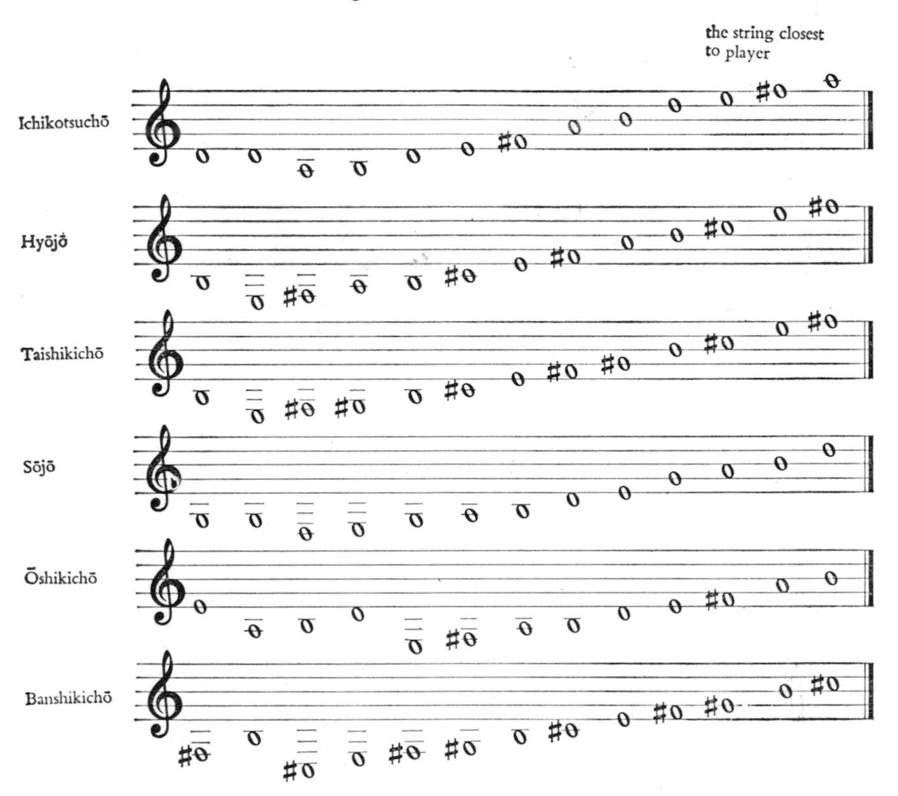

(iii) Percussion Instruments:

Kakko (Photos 13 & 14): A barrel drum with two skin heads. It is placed horizontally to the player on a stand and played with two sticks striking both heads. The basic and most characteristic patterns of rhythm are Katarai and Mororai as shown in Notation 6.
San-no-tsuzumi (Photo 18): A large hourglass drum with two skin heads. It is placed on the floor and held with the left hand. Only one head is struck.

Fig. 11 Notation 6

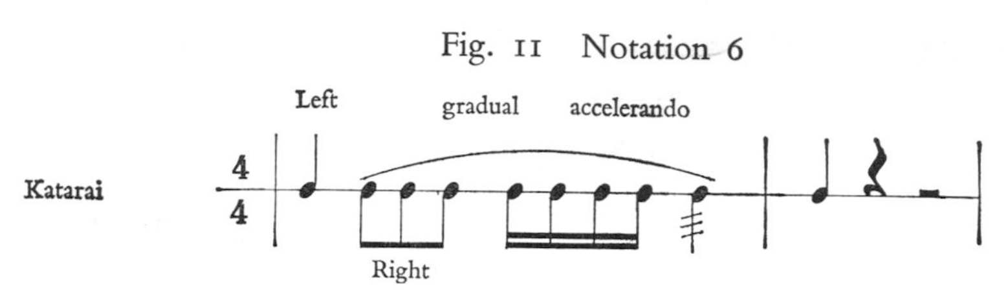

Mororai

Shôko or *Shôgo* (Photo 19): A round, bronze gong, hung in a frame on a stand. The size of the gong varies according to the style of music being performed. In the case of Bugaku the instrument is used in pairs and is played with two mallets.
Taiko (Photo 15–17): A large flat drum with two skin heads, hung in a frame on a stand. For Kangen it is smaller and called Gakudaiko, while for Bugaku it is gigantic in size, used in pairs and called Dadaiko. The gigantic drum for Bugaku has a loud, beautiful sound (Photos 15, 16 & 17).

A short explanation on the orchestral structure of (the left) Kangen, should be added here. The Hichiriki (oboe, Photos 5 & 6) plays the main line of melody, while the Ryûteki (flute, Photo 7) melody parallels that of the Hichiriki, with an occasional decoration in a kind of obligato style. The lowest note of each chord on the Shô follows the important point of the main melody. This means the chords hang over the melody, which is the reverse of modern Western music (monody) in which the melodic element is supported by the chord. Contrary to the Shô, the highest note of each chord on the Biwa and Sô follows the main point of the melody of the piece, as one might expect in monody. A harmonic structure where the melody is supported by harmony both from above and below, has not been found in any music of the world except Kangen.

Kangen and Bugaku are based on a tone system borrowed from the Chinese system of the T'ang dynasty. It consists of twelve tones (chromatic scale), two seven-tone scales, called Ryo and Ritsu and six tonalities called Rokuchôshi (Notation 7 & 8). The first three examples are in the scale of Ryo, while the remaining three are in the Ritsu scale. The keys

Fig. 12 Notation 7

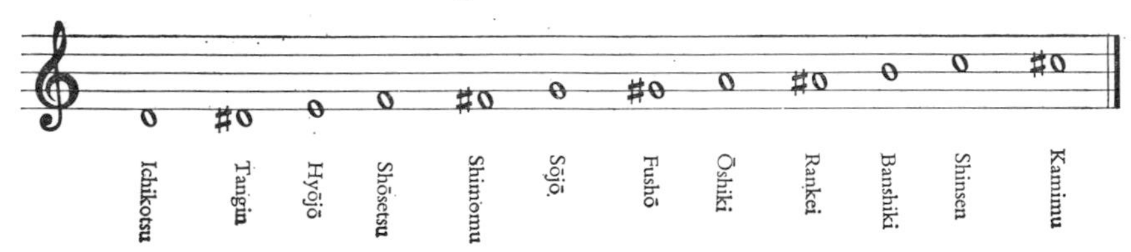

Fig. 13 Notation 8

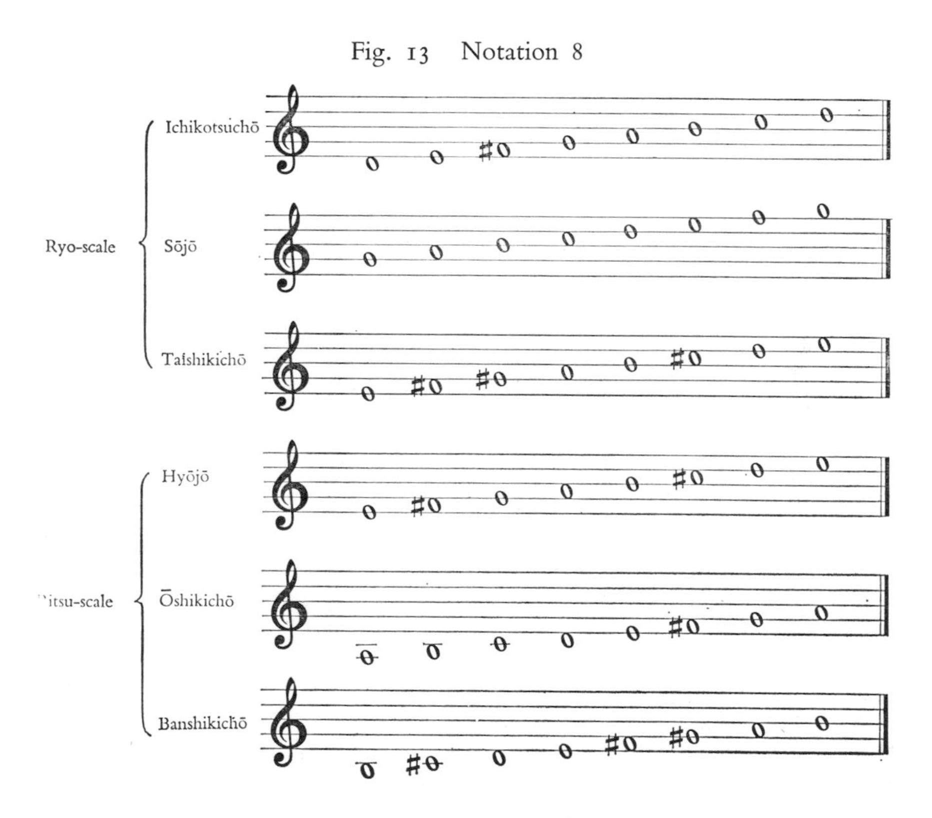

vary except Taishikichô and Hyôjô which are in the same key, d. Some of the names of these six tonalities come from the name of the note of the key. Names of the twelve tones are shown in Notation 7. Compositions of Kangen and Bugaku can be classified in three genres according to the size—small, medium and large.

The largest pieces consist of three movements, called Jo, Ha and Kyû, which can be translated roughly as (slow) introduction, (faster) development and (rushing) conclusion. The tempo is generally very slow and the difference between slow and fast does not vary to the extent of modern Western music.

The smallest piece consists of one movement, the parts of which are usually repeated in *da cappo* style. Performance of a piece or movement usually begins with a flute solo which is followed by a *tutti* at a certain given point.

Before performing a piece, as a rule, a short piece of the tonality to be used is played in a specific way. This is a stylized manner of tuning the instruments based on the fixed pitch of the Shô. It also serves as a warm up for the performer in the true atmosphere of the performance to follow.

Another noteworthy performance style is a kind of free style canon. In the performance of the Jo movement of (left) Bugaku, the chief Shô player starts by melody. Then the second Shô player starts by several beats, behind the chief player. He is followed by the third. The chief Hichiriki players joins in the Shô ensemble, then the second player behind him, and so on. The flutists join the ensemble in the same fashion. Thus the entire ensemble of three different wind instruments forms a free style canon in free rhythm creating a charming chaotic sound coupled with a marvelous dynamism.

The same performance style is found in six pieces, called Chôshi, (one piece for each tonality). Chôshi (as well as Jo) is used for the entrance of dancer or dancers on to the stage. The basic colour of costumes for a left dance is red, while for a right dance it is green. The number of dancers varies according to the piece—one, two, four, six and sometimes eight. Pieces performed by one dancer are rather special. In the left Bugaku most of such pieces originated in India, and the costumes for these dances are also specific, representing the survival of a non-Chinese origin.

(c) Songs

In the Gagaku concert, beside Kangen pieces, songs called Saibara and Rôei are performed. Saibara, literally means music of a pack-horse driver, and comprises songs composed in the Heian period, based upon contemporary folk songs modified in an artistic fashion. The existing repertoire of six pieces was restored in the Meiji era. The songs are accompanied by Ryûteki, Hichiriki, Shô, Biwa and Sô, while a leading singer beats time with a wooden clapper, Shakubyôshi. The Shô plays the melody instead of harmony.

Rôei, literally meaning chanting, is another type of song, the texts of which are taken from two collections of Chinese and Japanese poetry (*Wakan Rôei Shû* and *Shinsen Rôei Shû*). As in the case of Saibara, Rôei had once disappeared and fourteen pieces were restored in the Era of Meiji. The songs are accompanied by one Ryûteki, one Hichiriki and one Shô. The Shô plays the melody.

(d) Ritual music for Shintô ceremonies

This genre of Gagaku differs completely from the former three genres. It has its origin in ancient native music, and is used for ritual ceremonies of Shintôism at the Court and some shrines. The singing style as well as the instrumentation is also specific. The present-day performance style was established in the early Heian period. Styles of Kangen, Bugaku, Saibara and Rôei were also established. Slight influences can be traced from Kangen, Bugaku and Saibara in this ritual music, for instance, in the use of the Hichiriki.

There are four major pieces of this genre: Kagura, Yamato-mai, Kume-mai, and Azuma-asobi. Kagura is the largest piece of the genre. The term Kagura literally means "music of the gods." It is nowadays used also for folkloric ritual music at shrines, small and large, all over

Japan. This folkloric Kagura is often called Sato-kagura (country Kagura) or Okagura, while the Kagura in the court is named Mi-kagura. Mikagura is performed in the Court shrine with the attendance of the Emperor, on the 15th of December and in certain other cases of ritual ceremony. The complete ceremony used to take a few days to perform the many songs, some of which were accompanied with dance. Now, however, the ceremony is abbreviated to around six hours in the evening, and the performance of twelve songs (Photo 26).

The ensemble to accompany the songs consists of three instruments, Kagurabue (flute), Hichiriki and Wagon (zither), plus two Shakubyôshi (clappers), played by the lead singer from the two choruses.

The Kagurabue, literally meaning Kagura flute, is a transverse bamboo flute with six finger holes, producing a (closed), d', e', f', g', a', and c''. The Hichiriki is the same as previously mentioned. The Wagon or Yamatogoto, literally meaning Japanese zither, is a six-stringed long zither, six feet and four inches in length. Its silk strings are tuned by six

Fig. 14 Notation 9

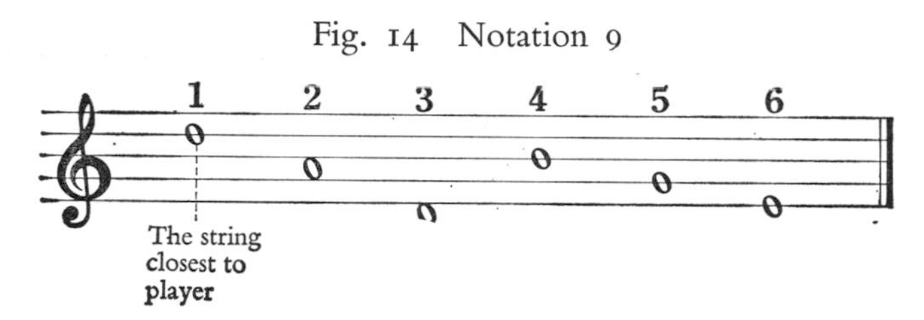

Fig. 15 Notation 10

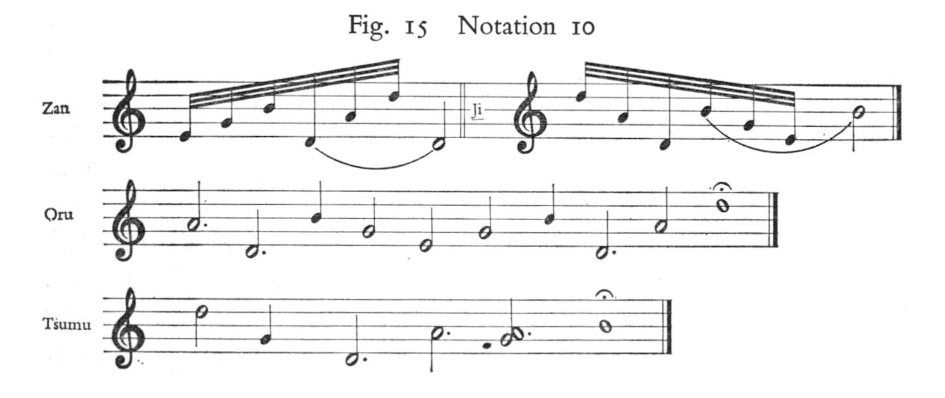

bridges made of natural branch (Notation 9). The strings are played with a thin plectrum shaped like a spatula and in four major patterns of melody (Notation 10, Photos 8, 27 & 28).

Yamato-mai, literally dance of Yamato (the older name of Japan), is a short piece performed by four or six dancers dressed in the ancient costumes of civil bureaucrats. The ensemble consists of Kagurabue, Hichiriki, Wagon and chorus. The chorus leader gives the beat with Shakubyôshi.

The Kume-mai, literally means dance of the Kume clan (a clan of ancient warriors called Kume). The dance is a short piece performed by four dancers dressed in the ancient costume of a court warrior. It is also accompanied by the ensemble of Kagurabue, Hichiriki, Wagon and chorus.

Azuma-asobi, literally play of the east country, is also a dance piece performed by four or six dancers dressed in the costume of court warriors of the Middle Ages. It is accompanied in the same manner as those previously mentioned. The song consists of four shorter pieces, the first and the second of which have no dance. In the dance, as well as the Kume-mai, instrumental music is played for the entrance and exit of the dancers.

(2) Shômyô (Buddhist Chanting)

The term Shômyô comes from the Chinese word Shêng-ming which stems from the Sanscrit, "Sabdavidya," meaning a course of study for linguistics, rhyme and vocalisation. This was one of the five major courses of study of Brahmanism, the prototype of Buddhism. When Buddhism was introduced to Japan, Buddhist chanting was called Bonbai, the Japanese pronunciation of the Chinese Fan-pei, literally meaning pure chanting. Later Shômyô took the place of Bonbai.

The history of Buddhist chanting in Japan began with the introduction of Buddhism around 552. However, Shômyô which has been preserved to today had its beginning in the Heian period when two Japanese priests, Saichô and Kûkai, brought Chinese chants from the mainland and established the Tendai sect and the Shingon sect respectively. These two sects have been responsible for the major kinds of Shômyô we know today. The Tendai sect has its headquarters in Enryakuji Temple on Mt. Hiei near Kyôto, and the headquarters of the Shingon sect was originally in the Tôji Temple of Kyôto, later moving to the Kôyasan Temple south of Ôsaka.

After the Kamakura period, several Japanese Buddhist sects, Jôdo, Shinshû etc., were established. It was at this time that Zen Buddhism was introduced and soon became a major sect. Each of these sects had their own system of chanting, based upon chants of the Tendai and Shingon sects.

Japanisation of Buddhist chanting proceeded from the Muromachi period at which time popular and pure Japanese chants using Japanese texts and hymns (Wasan and Goeika) were in fashion among the common people. Thus, Shômyô has been kept alive in Japanese life for a thousand years.

However, recently, Shômyô has become more and more formal as ceremonial music in the temple and at home, and has lost the power of real religious emotion. Most Japanese have forgotten the term Shômyô which was supplanted by the more popular term O-kyô (Buddhist text), which came to have a rather dull effect for most people. It is true that the texts are obscure to most except those priests in charge of the chants. Nevertheless, the performance of Shômyô in ceremonies in an authentic way still creates a memorable impression because of its accomplished style.

Buddhist chanting varies to a great extent according to purpose and sect. The language of the text varies into three major groups, Sanscrit, Chinese and Japanese. The tone system also varies. Some have a seven-tone mode, others a five-tone mode, and then there is a specific modal style based on the nuclear tone system similar to that of the Noh. Actually Shômyô influenced Noh and Heikebiwa to a great extent.

Each Buddhist ceremony (Hô-e) consists of many sections, which vary according to purpose and sect. The most conspicuous and large sections are Hôyô and Kôshiki. Hôyô are often placed at the beginning of a ceremony, having four lengths of duration. The largest is called Shika-nôhôyô and consists of Bai, Sange, Bon-non and Shakujô. Kôshiki was the ceremonial style in Japan in the middle of the Heian period (the beginning of the 12th century). It is chanted in Japanese. The melodic line of Kôshiki closely resembles Noh melodies. (Photos 40–44)

(3) Biwa Music

The Biwa which was used only as a member of the Gagaku ensemble in ancient times, began to be an instrument to accompany Buddhist chanting in the early Heian period. The music was called Jishinbiwa, since the text was the Buddhist text, Jishin-kyô. It was also called Môsô-biwa (blind priest biwa) where the cantor accompanied himself with the Biwa. Later Jishinbiwa moved to northern and southern Kyûshû, and has been preserved until today, although it has gradually become decadent. (Photo 46)

In the beginning of the Kamakura period, a new type of Biwa music called Heike-biwa appeared. It was a music narrating the Heike Monogatari (Tales of the Heike Family). This is one of the most representative examples of historical literature of the period, telling about the rise and fall of the Heike family, the greatest household of aristocrats. (Photo 45)

This Biwa music is most noteworthy as the first appearance of a narrative style of music in Japan, called Katarimono. The Biwa used in this music was almost the same as the Biwa of Gagaku, except smaller in size.

At the end of the Muromachi period, the Satsumabiwa appeared in the southern province of Kyûshû under the sponsorship of Lord Satsuma (the place name is now Kagoshima). This instrument was the successor of the Jishinbiwa in the province and of the Heikebiwa. The musical style became more rhythmical than the Heikebiwa, but it still retained the narrative style of the singer playing the Biwa only in the interval between the vocal parts. The manner of making the instrument was changed to some extent too.

During the Meiji era the Chikuzenbiwa appeared in the northern province of Kyûshû formerly called Chikuzen (Fukuoka since the Meiji era). This was the successor to the Môsôbiwa and the Satsumabiwa.

The music of the Chikuzenbiwa had a more brilliant, lyric style than the Satsumabiwa through the introduction of the techniques of Shamisen music and by being less narrative. After the Meiji era both Satsuma- and Chikuzen-biwa were brought to Tokyo. Then spreading throughout Japan, they established a major genre of traditional music complete with schools and differing sects (Photo 47).

The instruments, Satsumabiwa and Chikuzenbiwa differ from the Biwa of Gagaku to some extent. They have a smaller body, higher bridges, a softer front board, larger plectrum, thinner strings and a different playing method. The manner of holding the instruments also changed. With the Gagaku-biwa the instrument was held in a horizontal fashion, but the Satsumabiwa and the Chikuzenbiwa were held more vertically. The strings were stopped on the bridges with the Gagaku-biwa, but between the bridges with the Satsuma- and Chikuzen-biwa.

There are clear differences too between the Satsuma- and Chikuzen-biwa. The Chikuzenbiwa employs a smaller plectrum giving a softer sound, but at the same time it has a more brilliant melodic line which occurs not only between the phrases of singing, but together with the singing. The number of strings (four or five) and the tuning of both

Fig. 16 Notation 11

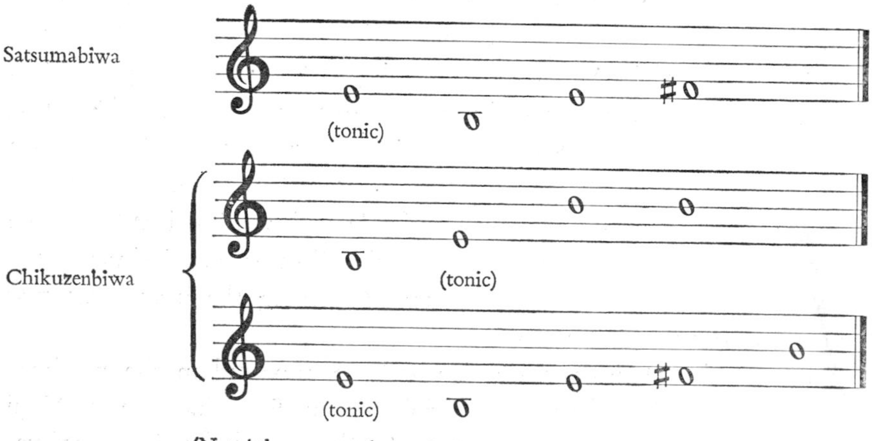

Satsumabiwa

(tonic)

Chikuzenbiwa

(tonic)

(tonic)

(Note: these notes do not indicate absolute pitch.)

schools vary according to the particular sect. The standard tuning method is indicated in Notation 11.

Because of the basic nature of narrative music, the music of these two Biwa created an epic style which does not have a specific musical form. It is more interesting, as in the case of the Heikebiwa, that both the singing and the instrumental interludes are based upon melodic patterns.

The singing patterns consist of two major styles, narrative style (*ji*), and the more melodic style (*fushi*). As a result of the history of the Satsumabiwa, which had its beginning in a Samurai society, the texts are concerned mainly with Samurai morals and historical stories of battle.

(4) Noh (Photos 30 & 31)

Despite the fact that Noh is essentially a theatrical art, its music is one of the most important genres of Japanese traditional music. This is true because the Noh is a representation of the highest synthesis of literature, theatre, dancing and music, where it is difficult to separate one from the other. Furthermore, the music represents one of the high points of Japanese music in that it had tremendous influence in the types of music which were to follow. Also, it must be pointed out that, despite the fact that the Noh is the art of the early Middle Ages, it remains alive in the minds of the Japanese today because its dignified and elaborate quality has refused to let the form die.

As to the history of the Noh, the first matter to be kept in mind is that all the stylistic features were set by the founders, Kan'ami Kiyotsugu (1333–1384) and his son, Zeami Motokiyo (1363–1443) who carried out this great work under the sponsorship of Ashikaga Yoshimitsu, the principal lord of the Muromachi period. Around one half of the 200 extant dramas, which have survived from an original répertoire of 2000 are the works of Zeami.

In the Muromachi period, Noh became not only more and more fashionable in the Samurai society, but was favoured by the common who were able to attend outdoor performances sponsored by temples.

Noh artists protected themselves by establishing their own guilds. In the Edo period, Noh was mainly sponsored by feudal lords and became formalized and ritualised, forgetting that the original spirit of the art was to entertain. However, in the Meiji era, the art was restored and revised into a high art form once again this time under the patronship of an aristocratic society together with wealthy businessmen.

In order to comprehend the music of the Noh, one has to understand the whole structure of the Noh, a perfect synthesis of drama, dance and music.

As shown in the illustration (Figure 19), the stage consists of the main stage, 570 cm square; a side stage for the chorus; a rear stage for musicians; and a long covered passage way which also serves as part of the stage. The entire stage is elevated 136 cm from the audience level and is viewed from two sides. A special acoustical device consists of several huge clay vases which are placed under the floor at designated points to create echo chambers (Photo 29).

On the rear wall of the musicians' stage, a huge pine tree is painted. No scenery or curtain is used on the stage save simple properties representing a house, tomb, boat, wagon, etc. Their shape and construction are simple and symbolic. The audience must have a lively imagination. In other elements of the Noh (acting, dancing and music) symbolism is the most important aesthetic. Costumes look in general sober, especially in colour, except for the gorgeous costumes of the principal actor to whom every element of the play and action of the stage is directed.

Actors are classified into three major divisions; Shite – principal actor, Waki – the second principal actor, and Kyôgen – comic relief actor. Actors from each division form groups and they do not switch from one division to another. Each division or group is divided into schools: Shite (five schools,—Kanze-ryû, Hôshô-ryû, Komparu-ryû, Kongô-ryû, and Kita-ryû), Waki (three schools) and Kyôgen (two schools). The Shite is the only major actor and as the central figure he dances and sings. Dialogue and monologue are rendered with a specific style of intonation. Most of the acting is formalized and from this attitude modified into dance. Singing and dancing, as well as the entrance and exit of the Noh drama is composed in one or two acts.

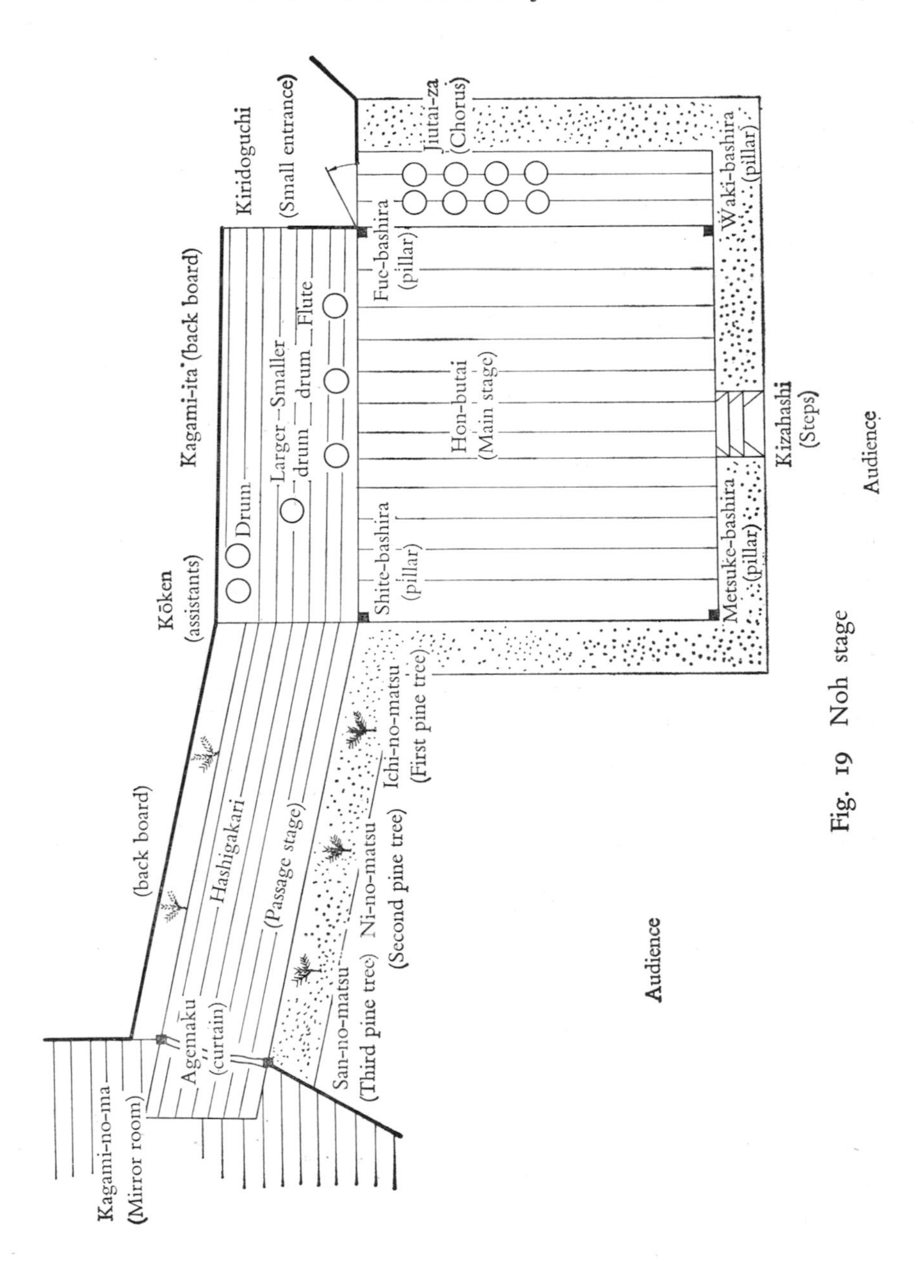

Fig. 19 Noh stage

The principal actor in a two act drama assumes a different role for each act. For instance, the actor may be a young woman in the first act and the ghost of a warrior in the second act. He goes backstage after the first act to change his costume, while the Kyôgen actor or actors perform on the stage. Then he returns.

The music of Noh consists of solo singing by the actors and chorus in unison, and an ensemble of four instruments, as well as monologue and dialogue. Although the construction of drama varies according to the plot, it is based upon a stereotyped form, which consists of sections placed in certain order. For example: (First Act) Shidai-Issei-Shodô-Kuri-Sashi-Kuse-Rongi; and (Second Act) Machiutai-Nochijite-Kiri. The dance section is inserted in either act or at times in both acts.

Each section of singing consists of stereotyped units, namely: *sage, haru, uki, mawashi, irikuri,* etc. The melodic line is one that mainly conveys the words and their meaning to the audience, but the severity of the melodic line is at times tempered with melissma. This type of singing might be compared in function to the recitative in western opera.

The tone system, as illustrated (Notation 12), consists of three main nuclear tones; high, middle and low. The interval formed between these tones is a perfect fourth. The lower tone serves as a final tone while the high tone occasionally may serve a final tone. In addition to the three nuclear tones mentioned, there exist two more tones of importance. The one a perfect fifth higher than the highest nuclear tone and the other a perfect fourth (or fifth) lower than the lowest nuclear tone. Of course, between these five tones other tones and intervals exist. Among them

Fig. 17 Notation 12

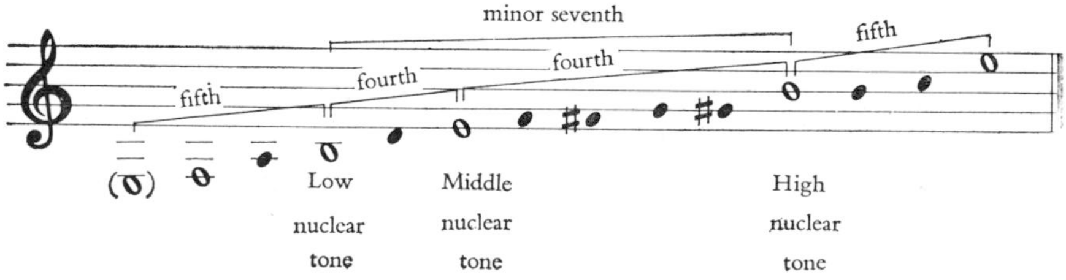

minor seventh
fifth
fourth
fourth
fifth
Low nuclear tone
Middle nuclear tone
High nuclear tone

the most important is the tone a whole tone higher than the highest nuclear tone.

There is a prescribed order for using these tones melodically. For example, the singer can never proceed directly from the highest nuclear tone to the middle nuclear tone (perfect fourth). It must be approached by going one whole step above the high tone and then to the middle tone (perfect fifth).

The most interesting aspect in the tonal system and melodic line is that between the highest and lowest tone the interval of a minor seventh exists. This would seem to indicate that the tone system is not one which is derived from the usual diatonic scale.

In addition, there are two styles of singing, soft and strong. In the soft singing, the tone system previously mentioned is the one used, while in the strong singing, the tone system shown by Notation 13 is the one used. Here the number of nuclear tones decreases to two and the interval between the two is a minor third.

Fig. 18 Notation 13

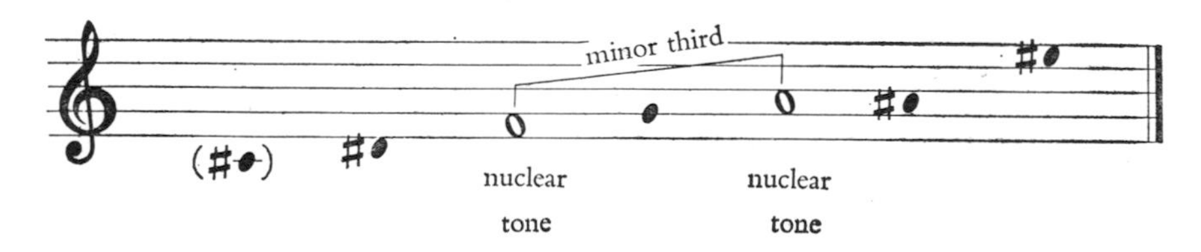

This is really a compressed style of the former tone system. Melodic lines move straight along on one nuclear tone and have much less movement than those of the former tone system.

Rhythm is the most important characteristic of Noh music. This is especially true regarding free rhythm. Basically, the rhythmic feature of both singing and the instrumental ensemble is the unit of eight beats. The singing text consists mainly of five or seven syllable phrases with some variation at times. These syllables are adapted to the eight beat structure by three specific rules—hira-nori, chû-nori and ô-nori. Hira-nori is the most specific and following this rule the second, fourth and eighth beats are prolonged to fit the seven-five syllable pattern. However, this type of fitted rhythm is not strictly adhered to in a metronomical sense, but is performed with elasticity and refinement.

The instrumental ensemble of the Noh theatre, while using four instruments at most, still gives a very strong impression because of the specific style of the ensemble and the special and refined timbre of each instrument. The transverse bamboo flute, Noh-kan (Photos 32–33) is the only melodic instrument other than the voice, but its melody is quite a different line from that of the singing. The flute has seven finger holes and the intervals, as well as absolute pitch, are rather vaguely fixed because the delicate changing of intonation is more important than the melodic line fixed by strict intonation.

The smaller drum, or shoulder drum, Ko-tsuzumi (Photos 34–35) is an hour-glass shaped drum with two horse hide heads, which are bound together by flaxen braids. The player holds the drum on his right shoulder and strikes the front skin with the fingers of the right hand in five degrees of strong and weak. The pitch of the drum (although an indefinite one) is regulated by tension of the hand ropes with the left hand, which in turn stretches or relaxes the membrane producing higher or lower sounds. The timbre it gives forth creates a profoundly beautiful effect. The player controls delicately the timbre by putting small and thin paper strips on the back skin of the drum. These help to take into account the humidity, temperature, size and shape of the hall where he plays.

The larger drum, an arm drum, O-tsuzumi (Photos 36–37), is a slightly larger hourglass shaped drum with two horse hide heads. The player holds it on the left knee with the left hand and strikes the front head with the middle finger of the right hand which is covered with a hard paper thimble. The skins must be pre-heated over a charcoal fire for an hour before every performance in order to give the characteristic sharp, dry sound.

Another drum, the Taiko (Photos 38–39), is a flat barrel drum with two cow hide heads. It is placed on a stand on the floor and played with two wooden sticks. The quality of sound of this drum depends upon the skill of lashing the two heads to the body. This procedure must be repeated by the player for every performance.

The rhythmic patterns of these drums are based upon the eight beat phrase and there are about two hundred patterns for each drum. These patterns are performed in combinations by applying certain rules which creates a truly remarkable rhythm resembling a mosaic. Most interesting is the sophisticated combination of free and fitted rhythm between the instruments of the ensemble itself, and between the ensemble and the singing.

In short, the basic, overall form of Noh music is highly stereotyped. Nevertheless, within this framework a great deal of elasticity exists. The all inclusive aesthetics of Noh were expressed by the founder, Zeami, as Yûgen (beauty, elegance and nobility) and Hana (flower or charm). The idea can be expressed in another word, symbolism. Noh can be regarded as a stage art which achieves one of the deepest and highest expressions possible in the theatre with the most economical use of materials.

(5) Sôkyoku (Koto Music) or Sankyoku (Photos 48 & 49)

This is one of the three major genres of the Edo period. Sô means Koto and Kyoku means music. The instrument, the Koto, originates in the previously mentioned Koto (Sô or Gakusô) of Gagaku. The Koto, in the Gagaku, is a member of the ensemble, but according to historical sources, in older times there were a number of solo pieces for the instrument.

In the later 16th century (Momoyama period) a Buddhist priest in northern Kyûshû, named Kenjun (1547–1636) composed the first songs to be accompanied by the Koto. This new music was called Tsukushi-goto, taking the name of the province where the priest lived. Then, a blind musician, Yatsuhashi Kengyô (1614–1685) of Kyôto learned Tsukushi-goto and created a new style of Koto music.

He imitated the musical form of Tsukushi-goto pieces which consisted of six short songs and named his style Kumi-uta (suite of songs).

The biggest difference between Tsukushi-goto and Yatsuhashi was in the tuning and mode employed. Tsukushi-goto used the tuning based on the *ryo*-mode (Notation 7) of Gagaku, while Yatsuhashi created tunings called Hirajôshi and Kumoi-jôshi (Notation 13) based on the *in*-mode (Notation 1) which have become the representative tunings and modes of the Koto since that time. Yatsuhashi and his successors composed some solo instrumental pieces, but most of the compositions for Koto are songs accompanied by the instrument.

Almost at the same time as the appearance of Tsukushi-goto, Shamisen music occurred in Japan, and Ikuta Kengyô (1656–1715) devised the

Fig. 20 Structure of the Koto

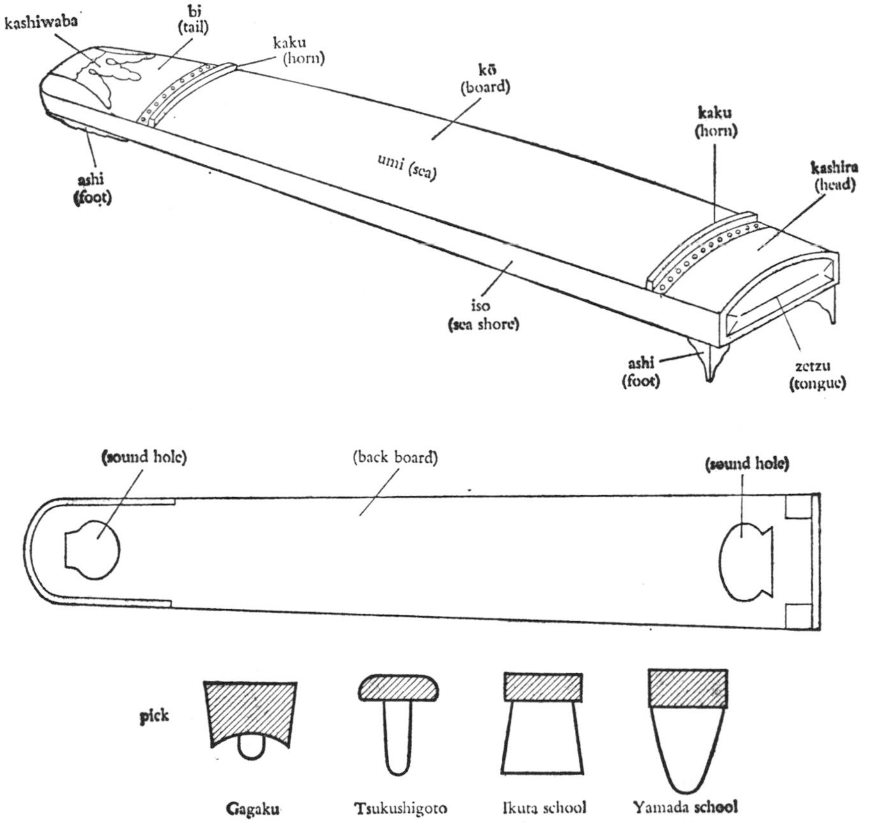

style of performing Ji-uta, a Shamisen music, together with the Koto. From that time instrumental interludes of songs accompanied by both instruments began to appear and many pieces began to consist of shorter parts of singing and longer instrumental parts—one to three in a song. This instrumental part, not merely an interlude any longer, was called *Te-goto* (hand-affair), and the style of these songs was *Te-goto-mono* (*Te-goto* style).

While the *Te-goto* style developed in Kyôto and Ôsaka, in Edo another new style of Koto music was established by Yamada Kengyô (1757–1817) who introduced the contemporary Shamisen music into Koto music.

Later at the end of the Edo period, Yoshizawa Kengyô in Nagoya created still another style-song accompanied by only the Koto which hinted at the oldest style of Koto music, Kumi-uta. The main point of difference between his style and the older Kumi-uta style was that he used poems (*waka*) from the famous anthologies of ancient *waka*, *Kokin Waka Shû*, *Kin Yô Shû*, etc. At the same time he created a new tuning quite different from the older tunings. His was based upon both the *In*-mode and the *Yô*-mode. The tuning called *Kokin-jôshi* (Notation 13) is taken from the name, *Kokin Waka Shû*.

Since Western music was introduced at the beginning of the Meiji Era, many attempts to change the older style were made with relatively little success. The first composer to combine Western music and Koto music was Miyagi Michio (1895–1956). He tried to introduce the diatonic scale, triple rhythm and orchestral style, which Japanese traditional music had never used before. Since then Miyagi's ideas have been favored by many Japanese musicians, many Koto players have imitated his style, while others, critical of his style have attempted to create other styles.

Recently, especially since the Second World War, composers trained in Western music in Japan began to join the movement for creating new styles based on the traditional styles.

The structure of the Koto (Figure 6) is almost identical to that of the Gakusô of Gagaku. It consists of one thick front board, 186 cm in length and 48 cm in width. Pawlonia wood used for the body is sufficiently soft for a silk stringed instrument and is of the proper size to facilitate the construction of the Koto. The back of the front board is hollowed out to which the thin back board of the same wood is affixed. Two sounding holes are bored out of the back board.

Thirteen silk strings, each of the same thickness, are strung between two thin, low bridges fastened near the ends of the instrument. Each string, however, is tuned by a movable bridge shaped as an inverted Y.

The player plucks the strings with three ivory picks fitted to the thumb, index and middle fingers of the right hand by bands. The shape of the pick differs between the two major schools of Koto music. In the Ikuta school a thin, square-shaped pick is used, while that of the Yamada school is thicker and rounded. The difference in the pick gives a delicate variation in timbre.

The Koto is the stringed instrument of Japan which produces the purest musical tone. However, because of the Japanese taste for the musical effects of noise, there are some special techniques for this purpose. For instance, scraping the strings would be one such technique which stands out in sharp contrast to the basic technique of plucking the strings.

When the Koto began to be accompanied by the Shamisen, the previously mentioned Tegoto style (instrumental) came in to fashion. The polyphonic ensemble of Koto and Shamisen or of two Kotos became popular. The first Koto part is called Hon-te and the secondary part is called Kae-de. Kae-de is often a more sophisticated melodic line. When a third part joins the two Kotos it is in the style of a drone or ostinato. The Shamisen part is also added to the Koto ensemble to produce a quasi-polyphonic effect.

Since the end of the Edo period, the Shakuhachi, a vertical bamboo flute is the third instrument to be added to the Koto and Shamisen. This is called Sankyoku (Photo 48), literally meaning, three compositions, but in this case signifying three instruments.

In older times, another stringed instrument, the Kokyû (Photo 53), was used in the ensemble in place of the Shakuhachi. The Kokyû as previously explained is the only lute played with a bow. It is shaped like the Shamisen but much smaller and played with a bow like that of a violin. The musical form of Koto compositions varies according to the historical styles previously mentioned. Most of the pieces are songs. The oldest style, Kumi-uta, is a song style consisting of six short songs. The texts concern a certain subject, but do not have what might be called a plot. The most arresting feature of the form is its archaic manner. Each song has the same number of measures (32), and the first measure of each four measures is a stereotyped Koto pattern. Every song ends with another pattern. In the pieces composed later, however, these stereotyped patterns gradually disappeared.

Kumi-uta was sung and played by one musician. This manner of performance, that singer and player are to be one and the same, has been preserved today as the traditional manner of performing Koto music.

At the same time as the appearance of Kumi-uta, some instrumental pieces were composed in a style called Dan-mono or Shirabe-mono. Dan means section and Shirabe means instrumental piece. The oldest piece of this kind is Rokudan-no-shirabe (Instrumental piece of Six Sections). This piece is a kind of free style variation and each section has the same number of measures (26).

Tegoto-mono, which occupies a big part of the Koto repertoire, are songs with long instrumental sections (*tegoto*). The number of instrumental parts vary from one to three. Usually a song is composed in three sections; beginning song (Mae-uta), *tegoto*, and the final song (Ato-uta). The largest piece is constructed with the following form of seven sections: song (Mae-uta)—Tegoto—song (Naka-uta)—Tegoto—song (Naka-uta)—Tegoto—song (Ato-uta). An example of this style, Nebiki-no-matsu, has an instrumental introduction in addition to the parts mentioned, and the composition requires 35 minutes to perform. The form of a song without Tegoto varies according to the plot and subject. Basically, however, these forms are based upon the idea of three sections —Jo-Ha-Kyû which have been previously mentioned.

Most of the Koto songs are elegant, lyric poetry as the Koto was enjoyed mainly by women at home. Even love affairs and emotions are expressed in a refined way, while with the Shamisen they are more dramatic and realistic. A number of the Yamada School's pieces for Koto and Shamisen are written in a more dramatic style, but still they are performed less dramatically than Shamisen music.

Beside the Koto, some other long zithers were devised in the Edo period. Photo 76 shows one of them, called Yakumo-goto, having two strings and no bridge to tune. This is a variation of the ancient Chinese seven-stringed zither (Ch'in).

(6) Shamisen Music (Photos 54, 55 & 57)

The Shamisen is a three-stringed lute-like banjo. It is the Japanese modification of the Chinese San-hsien (three strings) which appeared in China in the Yüan dynasty (13th century) under the influence of Qubuz or Setar of Islamic West Asia. The Chinese San-hsien was introduced to the Ryûkyû Islands, southwest of Japan, where the instrument was in turn brought to Japan ca. 1562. The San-hsien and the San-shin of Ryûkyû is covered with snake skin, while the Japanese Shamisen uses cat or dog skin.

Other Japanese modifications of the instrument, together with a different playing method, has brought about significant changes in the style of the music which is shown in Chart 4. As shown in the chart depicting the geneology of Shamisen music, the style of its music can be classified into three major groups: Uta-mono (singing style), Katari-mono (narrative style) and Minyô (folk song).

Minyô which is primarily in the singing style accompanied by Shamisen makes up the third genre, although some folk songs are in the narrative style and the basic nature of folk song is separate from other Shamisen art music. Because the geneology on the chart can not be explained briefly, only the major genres which are in fashion today will be described here.

The oldest style of Shamisen art music was Shamisen-kumi-uta. As in the case of Koto-kumiuta, each piece is a set of several short songs accompanied in this case by the Shamisen. It should be pointed out that

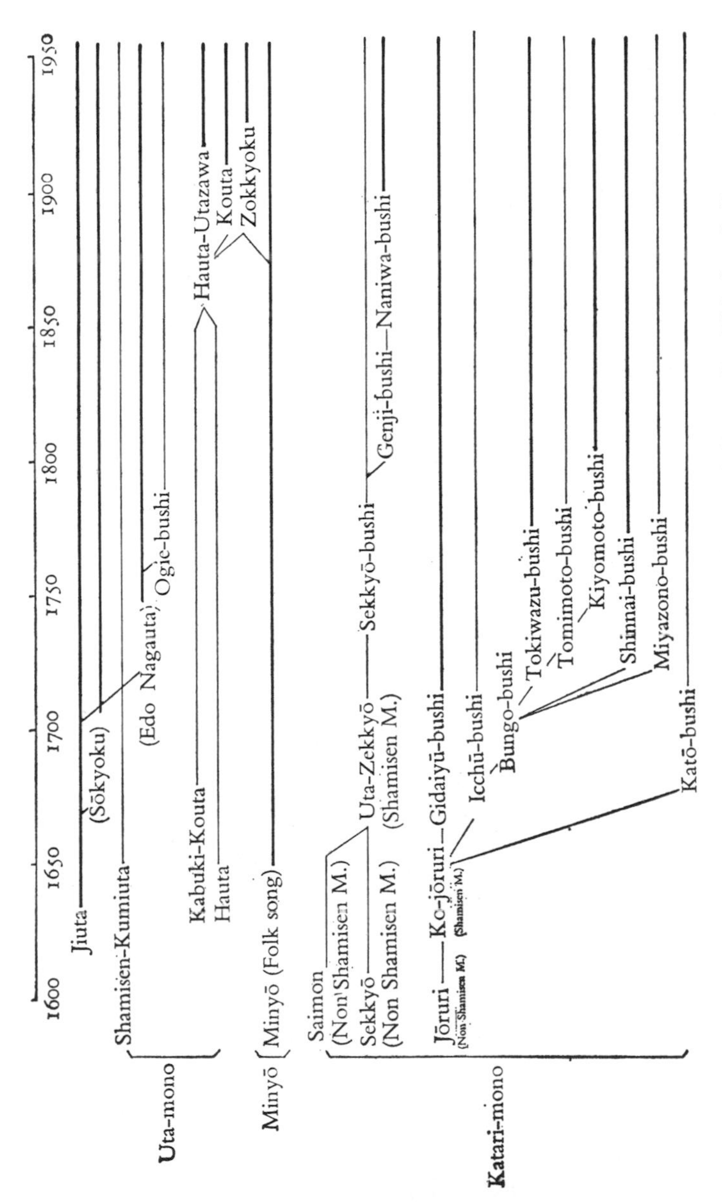

Notes: Thick lines indicate genres which are in fashion today. Thin lines indicate genres which are less in fashion today.

Chart 4 Genealogy of Shamisen

singer and player are one and the same. This style appeared in the area of Ôsaka and Kyôto where it was called generally Kamigata as mentioned earlier, and it is the older of the two main branches, Kamigata and Edo (present Tokyo), of Shamisen music. Shamisen-kumiuta was succeeded by Ji-uta, literally meaning local songs of the Kamigata area. As mentioned in the section of Sôkyoku, Jiuta was combined with Koto and developed into the Tegoto-mono, while both Jiuta and Tegoto-mono were also composed with only Shamisen accompaniment.

A Shamisen player of the Kabuki Theatre in Ôsaka, named Sakata Hyôshirô came to Edo to participate at the Kabuki theatre with Shamisen music resembling the early style of Ji-uta. This actually created a new style in the Edo Kabuki and was called Naga-uta, meaning long song, which became more and more brilliant and took over as the major music of Kabuki, accompanying mainly dance programmes. It has rather long instrumental interludes, and is accompanied by the Hayashi ensemble of Noh instruments (flute and three kinds of drums). This music uses a large number of singers, Shamisen players (in two parts, Honte, and Kaede or Uwajôshi) and Hayashi players (at times 30 members), who sit in specific costumes on a red-covered platform, giving a spectacular audio-visual effect (Photos 54 & 61). In addition, another group of musicians (a few singers and Shamisen players, about ten flute players, and many percussion instrumentalists) perform background music which has a marvellous atmospheric effect on the stage. They are called Geza-bayashi or Kage-bayashi, because they are hidden in the left end of the stage (Photos 62–69).

The second major genre, Katari-mono, is the most characteristic of Japanese music and has a fascinating style of vocal music not found in European music. Katari-mono means narration style. It is also called Jôruri, because the forerunner of Shamisen music was in narrative style and began with a story of a young lady named Jôruri. However, at first the story of Jôruri was not accompanied by the Shamisen. In the beginning of the Edo Period a pioneer of narrative Shamisen music whose name is unknown appeared in Kamigata. He was followed by many others among whom was Takemoto Gidayû (1651–1714) who established a new Jôruri named Gidayû-bushi for a puppet theatre (later called Bunraku) in cooperation with Chikamatsu Monzaemon (1653–1724), the most famous writer of drama for the Kabuki and puppet theatre. The term *bushi* means primarily melody or tune, but here it refers to style or school of Jôruri, as the general name of narrative Shamisen music. (The term *bushi* will be abbreviated as the term is repeated many times or is not necessary.) (Photos 56 & 57.)

Gidayû has been dominant in the field of Jôruri in Kamigata, while in Edo, Katô-bushi and Itchû-bushi became the major music of Edo Kabuki. Itchû originated in Kyôto and moved to Edo keeping the mood of Kamigata. The predecessor of Katô also originated in Kamigata, but it developed in the Edo mood, which was much brighter than that of Kamigata. Shortly after the mature period of Katô and Itchû, another style of Jôruri appeared in Edo, Bungo-bushi, which originated in Kamigata, and had a sudden success in Edo. However, because of overly sensational texts and their strong influence upon the people, it was prohibited by the Government of the Tokugawa Shogunate. Bungo-bushi was followed by two of its students who established Tokiwazu-bushi and Shin-nai-bushi. A pupil of the founder of Tokiwazu then established Tomimoto-bushi which was succeeded by Kiyomoto-bushi. These successors of Bungo-bushi took the place of the older Edo Jôruri, Icchû and Katô, on the stage of Kabuki, except Shin-nai which was in fashion outside of the Kabuki stage, mainly in the gay quarters.

Soon after the appearance of Kiyomoto, Tomimoto disappeared from Kabuki under the pressure of Kiyomoto and Tokiwazu. Thus, among the many kinds of Edo Jôruri, only Tokiwazu, Kiyomoto and Shinnai have survived as major genres of narrative Shamisen music, together with Gidayû from Kamigata.

At the end of the Edo period another genre of singing style Shamisen became fashionable among the lower classes of Edo. The music, Ha-uta, meaning short song was the revival of older popular songs from the beginning of the Edo period. A retired Samurai devised a more sophisticated and elegant type of song by using the same text. This was called Utazawa. Soon after, as a reaction to the heavy mood of Utazawa, a newer, shorter and more popular song, called Ko-uta (small song) appeared, which became the most popular of the three. It is noteworthy, that despite the current tendency of decay in the traditional music of Japan, Ko-uta was revived after the Second World War to a remarkable extent, especially among wealthy businessmen.

Zokkyoku (popular tune) is another genre of popular song accompanied by Shamisen. This genre covers miscellaneous popular songs which originated in order country popular songs, or folk songs. It was then refined to suit city life.

Finally, another type of Shamisen music should be mentioned because of its tremendous popularity. It is called Naniwa-bushi. It belongs to the narrative style and originates in Sekkyô-bushi, a combination of very old Jôruri narrating every day news and Gidayû. The name comes from the name of the place Naniwa (present Ôsaka) where the music was established. The style and text of Naniwa-bushi was most understandable and enjoyable to the people of the common class. It favored stories based upon older Japanese customs and virtues, ("obligation" and "human nature"). It is interesting to note that Naniwa-bushi began to decay after the Second World War because the American style of popular song took its place.

Quite a number of Minyô (folk songs) have been influenced by Shamisen music. This is especially true with the dominant mode of Shamisen music, the In-mode.

The Construction of Shamisen: (Photos 58 - 60)

The Shamisen (Fig. 21) in an instrument consistsing of four boards of Chinese quince or oak, through which a stick (88 cm long) made of red sandalwood or Indian red wood is inserted. The skin covering both sides of the body is usually cat skin, but in Gidayû thicker dog skin is used as well as in cheap practice Shamisens. A small piece of skin is glued on the front skin is to protect it from the striking of the plectrum. Three strings of different thicknesses are strung between pegs and the lower end of the stick which appears at the centre of the lower board of the body. The true length of the strings is determined by the upper gold bridge attached at the end of the peg-box and the lower bridge, made of ivory, water buffalo horn or wood, inserted between the string and the front skin. The lower bridge varies in size and weight according to the genre of the music, giving a variety of timbre of a delicate, but distinguishable difference. The strings are struck and plucked by a plectrum shaped in the form of a leaf from the Ginko tree. The shape, size and weight of the plectrum also varies according the genre of music, giving quite a remarkable variety of timbre. These variations of timbre are a very important element of Shamisen music.

Fig. 21 Structure of the Shamisen

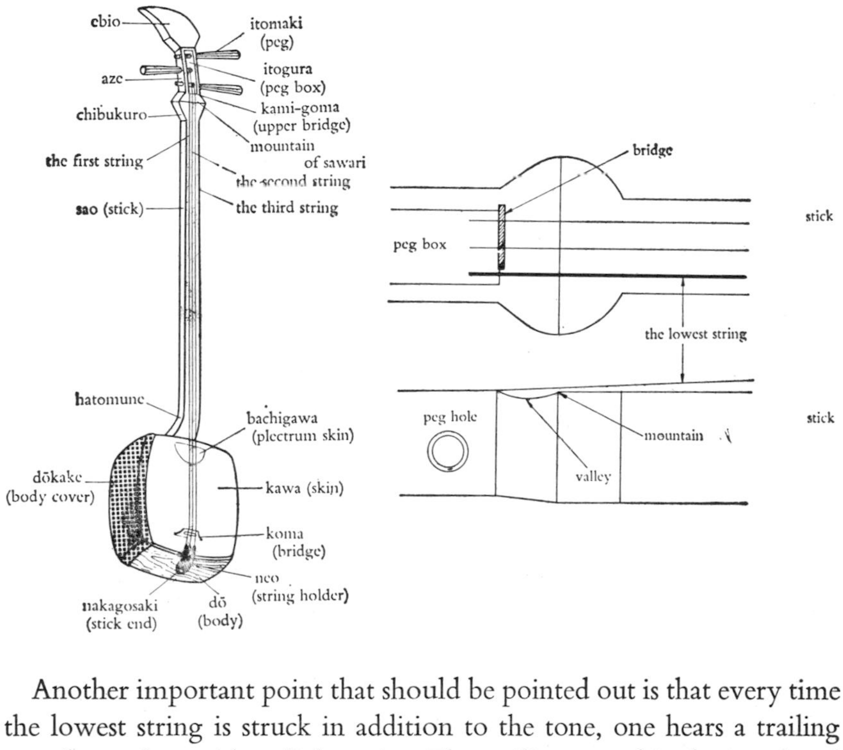

Another important point that should be pointed out is that every time the lowest string is struck in addition to the tone, one hears a trailing sound together with a slight noise. The trailing sound is also produced when the other strings resonate with the lowest string, especially when the intervals between the tone of the string played and the tone of the lowest string are an octave, two octaves, three octaves, a fifth, a fourth, etc. In other words, intervals that are consonant. This trailing sound is called Sawari, literally meaning to touch, and comes from the overtone occurring at the top of the stick as shown in Figure 21. The lowest string which does not rest on the upper bridge touches slight at the point of the "mountain" toward the end of the vibration and produces overtones, the pitch of which is determined by the ratio of the length of two parts of the string, one between the mountain and the upper bridge, and the other between the "mountain" and the lower bridge on the skin. This Sawari is indispensable to a good Shamisen tone and every player, as well as every maker, takes great care in controlling the delicate tension of the string to produce the Sawari.

The Shamisen is played by striking and plucking the strings with the plectrum held in the right hand and by stopping the strings with three fingers of the left hand on the fretless stick. The strings are also set in motion by plucking with three fingers of the left hand. The thumb and small finger are not used.

To play Ko-uta and for other special purposes, such as practising, the index finger is used instead of the plectrum. The most characteristic point of playing the Shamisen is that the plectrum (or the fingers) strike the skin at the same time of striking the string. This use of the plectrum is a very important factor. There are many other important factors which determine the quality of sound, such as the thickness of the skin, strings and stick; the angle at which the plectrum (especially which part of the edge) strikes the string.

The following list (Chart 5) gives some points of major difference between the major genres. Column I shows the order from the thickest stick (Futo-zao) to the thinnest stick (Hoso-zao). However, as shown in Column VI, the order of the sound quality does not necessarily correspond to that of the stick because of other discrepancies (Photos 56 & 58).

The Shamisen is an instrument which primarily accompanies singing. As a rule, the melodic line of the Shamisen forms almost the same melodic

Chart 5 Variations of the Shamisen according to musical genres in Shamisen music

<table>
<tr><th>I</th><th>II</th><th>III</th><th>IV</th><th>V</th><th>VI</th></tr>
<tr><th>Stick
(thick~thin)</th><th>Skin
(thick~thin)</th><th>Bridge
(heavy~light)</th><th>String
(heavy~light)</th><th>Edge of plectrum
(thick~thin)</th><th>Sound quality
(heavy~light)</th></tr>
<tr><td>Gidayû 3cm</td><td>Gidayû</td><td>Gidayû 23g</td><td>Gidayû</td><td>Gidayû</td><td>Gidayû</td></tr>
<tr><td rowspan="3">Jiuta
Tokiwazu
Kiyomoto</td><td rowspan="3">Jiuta
Tokiwazu
Kiyomoto</td><td rowspan="3">Kiyomoto
Tokiwazu</td><td>Kiyomoto</td><td rowspan="2">Tokiwazu
Kiyomoto</td><td>Kiyomoto</td></tr>
<tr><td>Jiuta</td><td>Tokiwazu</td></tr>
<tr><td rowspan="2">Kouta
Nagauta</td><td>Nagauta</td><td>Jiuta</td></tr>
<tr><td>Kouta</td><td>Kouta</td><td rowspan="2">Kouta
Nagauta 3.75g</td><td>Jiuta</td><td>Nagauta</td></tr>
<tr><td>Nagauta
2.2cm</td><td>Nagauta</td><td>Tokiwazu</td><td></td><td></td></tr>
</table>

line as that of the singing, but the Shamisen makes the rhythmic feature of the melodic line of singing clearer by the strong beat of the plectrum. The most characteristic relationship between singing and the Shamisen, as in the case of Koto music, is that singing is a little ahead of the beat (approximately half a beat). This technique aims not only at more sophistication of contrast between singing and Shamisen, but also makes the text more audible and understandable.

The polyphonic feature of the instrumental ensemble can be most often heard in Ji-uta and Naga-uta which often have instrumental parts or interludes called Ai-no-te or Aikata. As in the case of Koto music, the original part is called Honte and the secondary part is called Kaede.

Notation 14 shows three major tunings. Generally saying Honchôshi represents the standard mood, while Niagari gives brighter atmosphere and Sansagari is effective for melancholic expression. In a piece tuning is often changed one or a few times according to the mood. Changing from Honchôshi to Niagari, by raising one whole tone on the middle string which means musically the modulation from tonic to dominant, has a strong effect in changing the mood, atmosphere and feeling. When the Niagari tuning is moved to Sansagari by raising one whole tone on the lowest string after the previous changing from Honchôshi to Niagari, this results in the tonic being raised one whole tone from the Honchôshi. This occurs fairly often.

Fig. 22 Notation 14

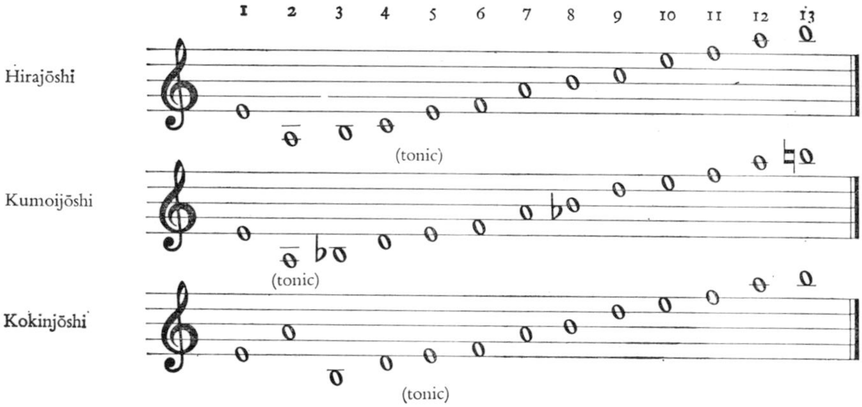

1 2 3 4 5 6 7 8 9 10 11 12 13

Hirajōshi

(tonic)

Kumoijōshi

(tonic)

Kokinjōshi

(tonic)

Fig. 23 Notation 15

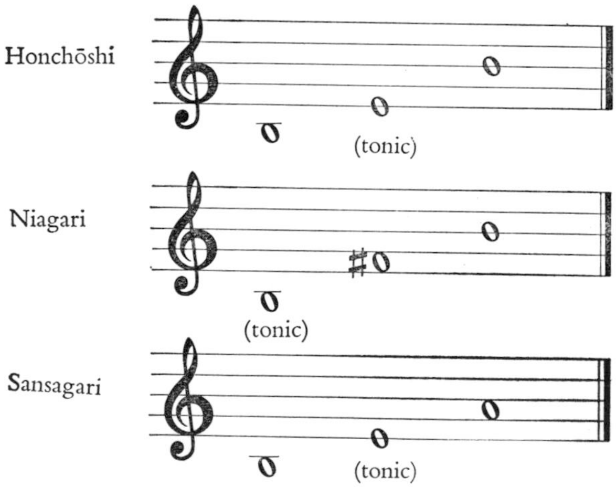

Honchōshi

(tonic)

Niagari

(tonic)

Sansagari

(tonic)

(Note: These notes do not indicate absolute pitch)

In Shamisen music, Uwajôshi is often used as the secondary part instead of Kaede. Uwajôshi, literally meaning high tuning or high pitch, is played on the Shamisen. A very small bamboo bar is bound to the stick together with the three strings in order to shorten the length of the strings by half. Usually this Shamisen has a different tuning from that of the original Shamisen part, and is played one octave higher. The polyphonic feature is very strong at times, for instance, in the simultaneous sounding of different melodies which are based on the tonic and subdominant keys.

The musical form varies with the genre. It is most noteworthy that the form of dance-drama of Kabuki accompanied by Naga-uta or Tokiwazu or Kiyomoto is influenced by Noh. A piece of this form begins with Okiuta (introductory song) which is followed by Michiyuki (literally journey—music for entrance of actors), then Mondô (dialogue), then Kudoki (literally love song—expression of emotion of the main actor), Odoriji (dancing) and Kiri (end). This stereotyped form corresponds to a great extent to that of the Noh drama.

(7) Shakuhachi Music (Photos 50 & 51)

In spite of its simple construction and the specific nature of its music, the instrument often charms western music lovers. The Shakuhachi is an end blown bamboo flute with four holes on the front and one on the back. The standard length of 1.8 Japanese feet (54.5 cm) is found in the name of the instrument—shaku-foot and hachi-eight.

In the Nara period, there was an end blown flute called Shakuhachi, but it had six finger holes, five on the front and one on the back. This was introduced from China and then disappeared in the Heian period. In the Muromachi period, another end blown bamboo flute from China, called hsiao, was brought to Japan and modified into the Hitoyogiri, literally meaning one joint bamboo. This is a smaller flute, 1.1 feet (33.3 cm) in length with five finger-holes. This was first favored by mendicant friars and later came into fashion among the lower class Samurai and merchants. (Photo 52.)

In the beginning of the Edo period itinerant Buddhist priests (Komusô) of the Fuke sect who were employed by Samurai began to use a 1.8 feet long Shakuhachi for their mendicancy. This was called the Fuke Shakuhachi.

A retired Samurai, Kurosawa Kinko (1710–1771), who was the teacher at a temple of the sect, established a style of art music on the instrument by composing new pieces based upon the repertoire of the Fuke Shakuhachi.

At the end of the Edo period musicians of the Kinko school began to participate in the ensemble of Koto music, taking the place of the previously mentioned Kokyû, together with the Koto and Shamisen. The repertoire of the original solo pieces of the Kinko school is called Honkyoku (original pieces) while the repetoire of Koto pieces in which the Shakuhachi participates is called Gaikyoku (outside pieces).

Since the Shakuhachi began to be played with the Koto, it became fashionable with men of every social class and in the middle of the Meiji Era (1896), Nakao Tozan established another school. Today the Kinko and Tozan schools dominate Shakuhachi music. The Fuke Shakuhachi declined since the Fuke sect was abolished by the Meiji government in 1871, when the organization for protection of blind Koto musicians, called Shokuyashiki, was also abolished.

The instrument is made from the lowest section of the bamboo. The average diametre of the pipe is 4–5 cm, and the inside of the pipe is almost cylindrical. The length varies according to the pitch of the ensemble of Koto and Shamisen. A difference of 3 cm renders a half tone. The standard length of 1.8 (Japanese feet) or 54.5 cm is used for solo pieces and the pitch of the open pipe, d, is regarded as the standard pitch. Five fingerholes, four in front and one on the back, give the following six tones in the standard pipe, d (closed), f, g, a, c, d'. By various fingerings, half holing, and controlling the angle of the mouthpiece against the lip, all of the twelve tones can be produced. The mouthpiece at the top of the pipe is made by cutting the edge diagonally toward the outside.

This type of mouthpiece makes it possible for the player to control the pitch by changing the angle, which in turn produces a delicate change in intonation not possible on a Western recorder (Blockflöte) having a whistle type of mouthpiece.

As well as the delicate changing of intonation and various kinds of portamento, the noise of blowing on the edge of the mouthpiece creates an artistic effect. Of course the mellow timbre of the rather thick bamboo pipe is the basic characteristic of the instrument. To give the best possible sound the inside of the instrument is carefully lacquered, as in the case of the transverse flutes of Gagaku and Noh.

The musical form of solo pieces (Honkyoku) does not show fixed forms. Different melodic lines are placed in a row. Many stereotyped interval units occur here and there.

The more important musical element is free rhythm. There is no piece of Honkyoku that is written in a fixed rhythm. The basic mode is the In-mode, the most common mode of Shamisen and Koto music.

The Honkyoku pieces of the Fuke sect (30 to 40 pieces) are based on the religious ideas of Zen Buddhism. Honkyoku of the Kinko School took over the repretoire of the Fuke Shakuhachi, but modified it into a more artistic style. Then, too, new compositions not religious in nature were added to the repertoire of the Kinkoryû Honkyoku (36 pieces).

(8) Folk Songs and Folk Music (Photos 70–75)

Despite the fact that contemporary life in Japan is modernized to a great extent both in the cities and country, much traditional folk song, music and drama has been preserved. Even work songs which are easily lost because of changing conditions have been kept alive as entertainment for feasts or parties. Numerous religious rituals, festivals and feasts are the background for such songs, music and drama. Some of them survive in the original primitive style based upon shamanism, animism, totemism and magic. Many of them have undergone a change because of historical development and because of the influence of art music—especially Shamisen music.

Folk songs in Japan can be classified according to their categories, as follows:

a. Work songs. For example, fishing songs, boatmen songs, pack-horse drivers' songs, rice planting songs, wine *(sake)* makers' songs, etc.
b. Bon Dance Songs. Most common throughout Japan as a Buddhist event in summer (urabon).
c. Songs for entertainment at feasts or parties.
d. Songs for weddings and funerals.
e. Children's songs and cradle songs.

As to the musical style, the most primitive style is in "Enge Melodie" (narrow melody), the compass of which does not reach an octave, and is often based upon a nuclear tone system. In-mode and Yô-mode (see Notation 1) are the dominate modes. Yô-mode (a five-tone system without semi-tone) is most characteristic of the more naive songs, while In-mode (a five-tone system with a semi-tone) is common among folk songs which have been influenced by Shamisen music, although it should be stated that songs of both types are often accompanied by the Shamisen.

As to rhythm, there are two types, free and fitted. Fitted rhythm (usual mechanical rhythm) is common in rhythmic work songs, dance music and songs, and children's play songs. Free rhythm occurs at times in work songs, entertainment songs unaccompanied or accompanied by the Shakuhachi instead of the Shamisen and drums. Drums of various kinds, huge and small, barrel and hour-glass shaped, played with sticks or without sticks, etc., are another important element. Often a transverse bamboo flute, as well as gong, bell and clapper make up the ensemble with the drums. This kind of ensemble is generally called Hayashi, which is the name of the instrumental ensemble of Noh and Kabuki previously mentioned. Hayashi (*hayasu* as a verb) primarily means to play and cheer up. Among the numerous kinds of folk music, the largest genre is called Kagura (God music). This folkloric Kagura, called O-Kagura, is completely different from the Kagura of Gagaku which is called Mikagura. O-Kagura occurs often at country shrines and is called Sato-Kagura (country Kagura). Although it varies to a great extent in style, the basic instrumentation of the ensemble is a transverse bamboo flute, drum of medium size, and often a big barrel drum.

Some folk songs of a certain locale have found their way to neighbouring villages, towns, and provinces, at times far from the place of origination. In this case, the style is changed to some extent. Folk songs have rapidly spread all over Japan because of records, radio and TV. In this spread through the mass media, the music has become commercial and the style of the music has changed to one of more artistry and refinement being performed by professionals. At any rate folk music or songs brings nostalgia to the man whose province or village has produced the particular music or song. For example, the author feels strong nostalgia in Kandabayashi since he was born and raised in Kanda of Tokyo.

References

Hisao Tanabe, Japanese Music, Kokusai Bunka Shinkokai, Tokyo, 1959. 74p.

Katsumi Sunaga, Japanese Music, Japan Tourist Bureau, Tokyo, 1936. 66p.

Genjiro Masu and Hideo Tanabe, Japanese Music, UNESCO Nippon, Tokyo, 1953. 78p.

William P. Malm, Japanese Music and Musical Instruments, Charles E. Tuttle, Rutland, Vermont and Tokyo, 1959. 299p.

F. T. Piggott, The Music and Musical Instruments of Japan, London, 1909.

H. Müller, Einige Notitzen über die Japanische Musik, Mitteilungen der Deutschen Gesellschaft für Natur-und Völkerkunde Ostasiens, I, fasc. 6, 1876.

Hans Eckardt, Japanische Musik, in Musik in Geschichite und Gegenwart (German Encyclopedia of Music), Baerenreiter-Verlag, Kassel und Basel.

Kashô Machida, Japanese Music and Drama in the Meiji Era, Vol. III of Japanese Culture in the Meiji Era edited by Dr. Toyotaka Komiya, Ôbunsha, Tokyo, 1956. 535p.

Shigeo Kishibe, Chapter on music in K.B.S. Bibliography of Standard Reference Books for Japanese Studies with Descriptive Notes, Vol. VI (B), Kokusai Bunka Shinkokai, Tokyo, 1960. p.121～172.

Robert Garfias, Gagaku, Theatre Arts Book, New York, 1959. 34p.

William P. Malm, Nagauta the Heart of Kabuki Music, Charles E. Tuttle, Rutland, Vermont and Tokyo, 1963. 344p.

Elizabeth May, The Influence of the Meiji Period on Japanese Children's Music, University of California Press, Berkley and Los Angeles, 1963. 95p.

Eta Harich-Schneider, The Rhythmical Patterns in Gagaku and Bugaku, E. J. Brill, Leiden, 1954. 109p.

Hans Eckardt, Das Kokonchomonshû des Tachibana Narisue als musikgeschichitliche Quelle, Otto Harrassowitz, Weisbaden, 1956. 432p.

Curt Sachs, Rise of Music in the Ancient World East and West, W. W. Norton, New York, 1943. 324p.

Gagaku ensemble (Kangen)

›n the stage of the Music Department
the Imperial Palace.

2. Bugaku performance (Right Dance)
On the stage of the Music Department
in the Imperial Palace.

3. Shô player

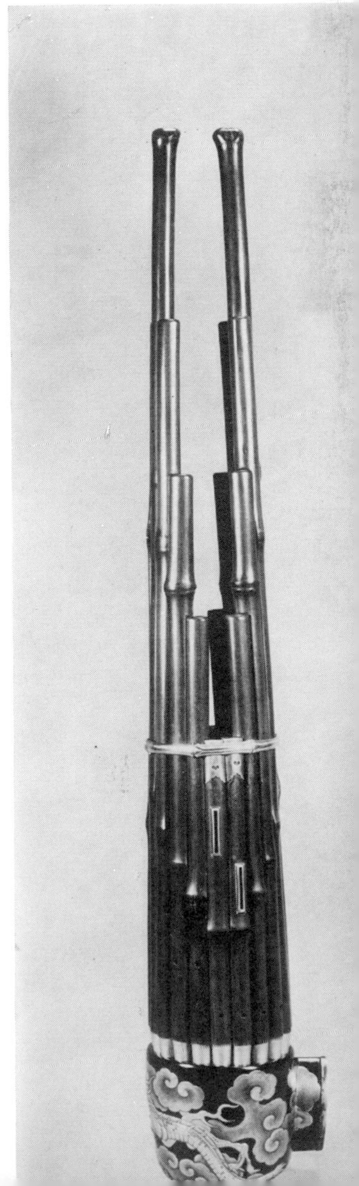

4. Shô

5. Hichiriki player

6. Hichiri

7. Ryûteki player

8. Kagurabue, Ryûteki, and Komabue

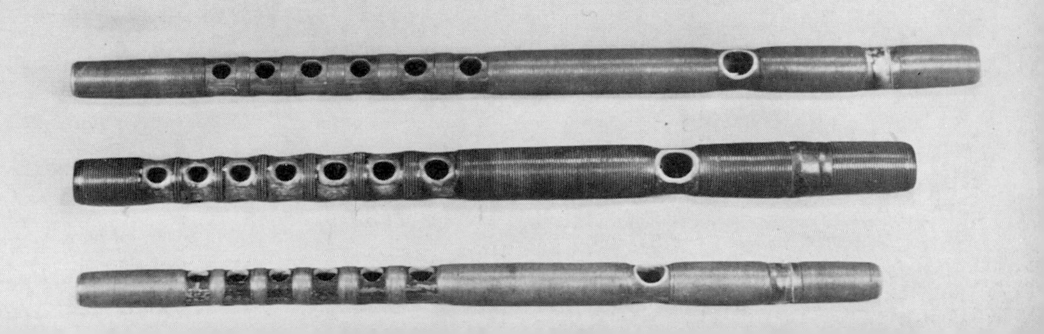

9. Biwa player

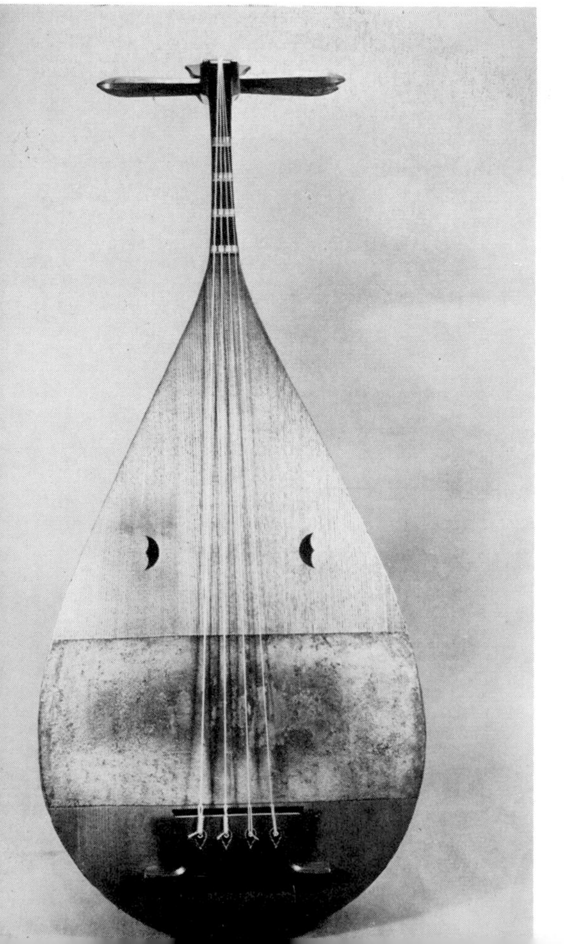

10. Biwa

11. Gakusô (Koto) player

2. Gakusô (Koto)

13. Kakko player

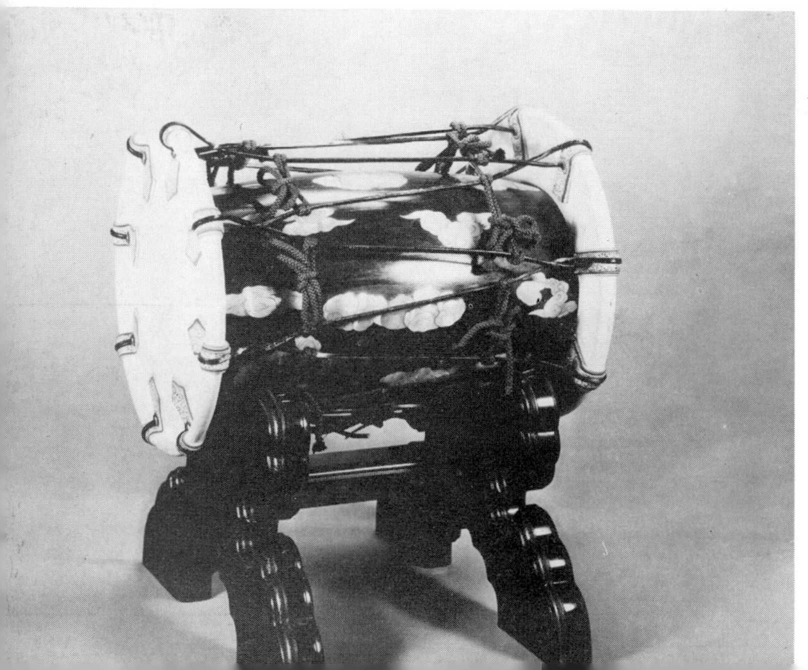

14. Kakko

15. Gakudaiko (Taiko) player

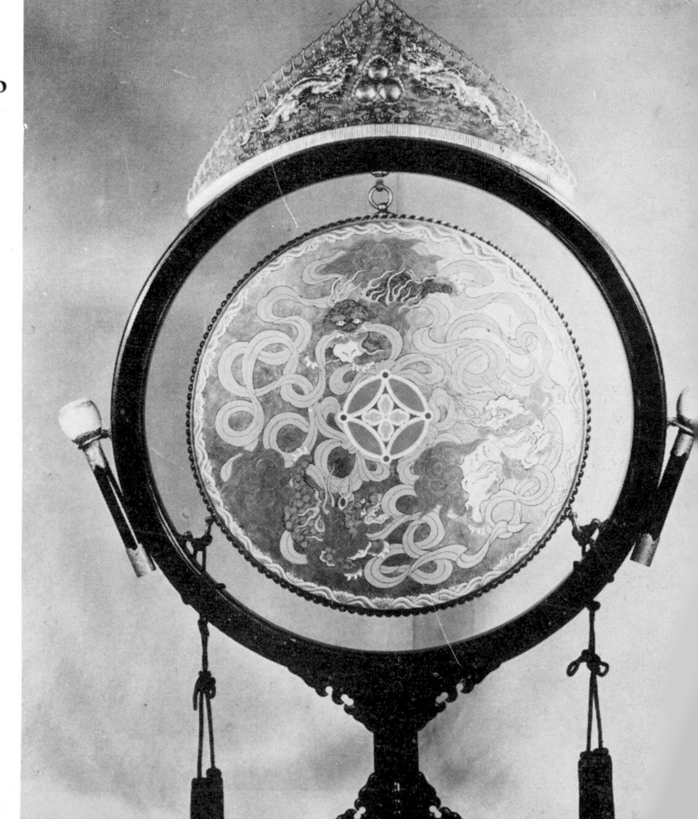

16. Gakudaiko

7. Dadaiko

3. San-no-tsuzumi

19. Shôko

20. Keirôko

21. Tôko (Furi-tsuzumi)

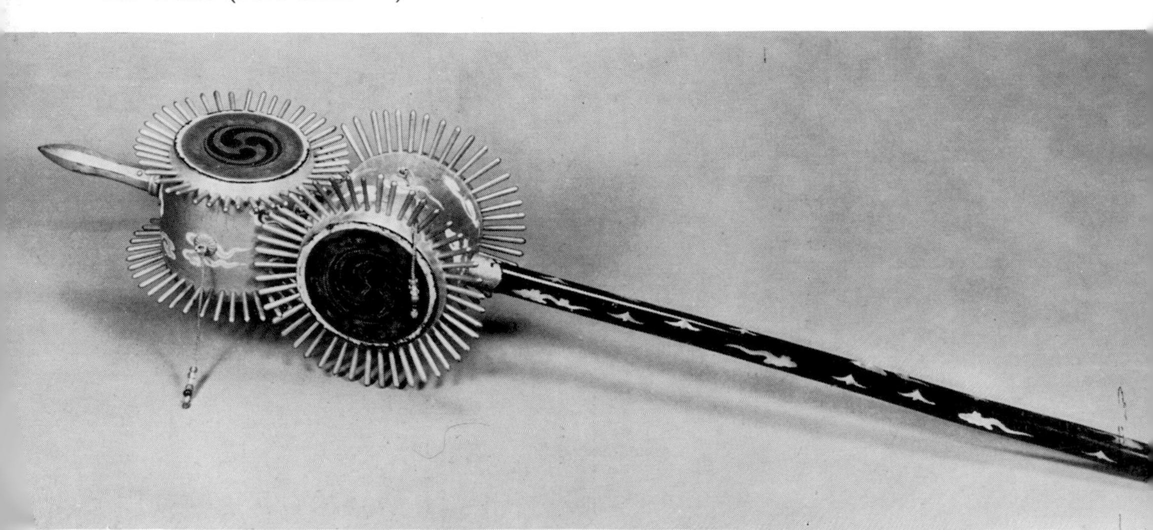

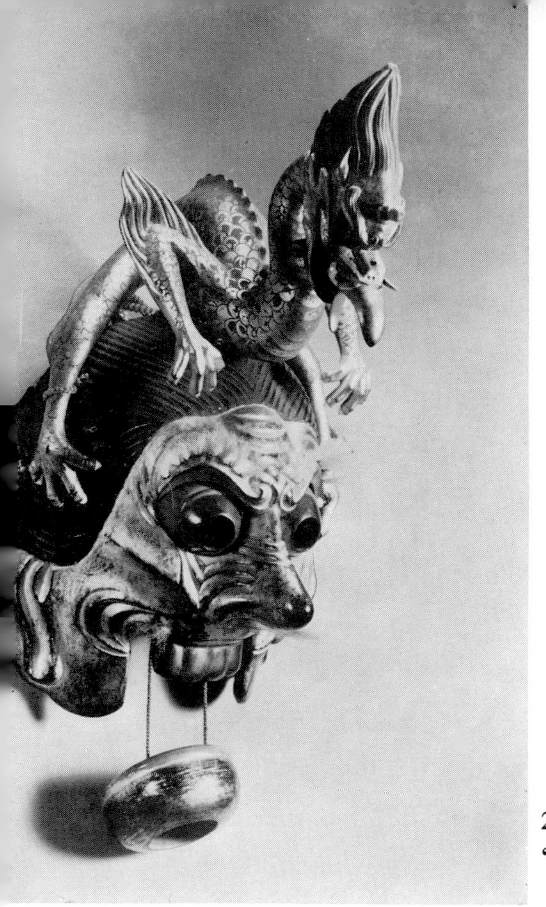

22. Bungaku mask (Left Dance): "Ranryô-ô"

23. Bungaku mask (Left Dance): "Genjôraku"

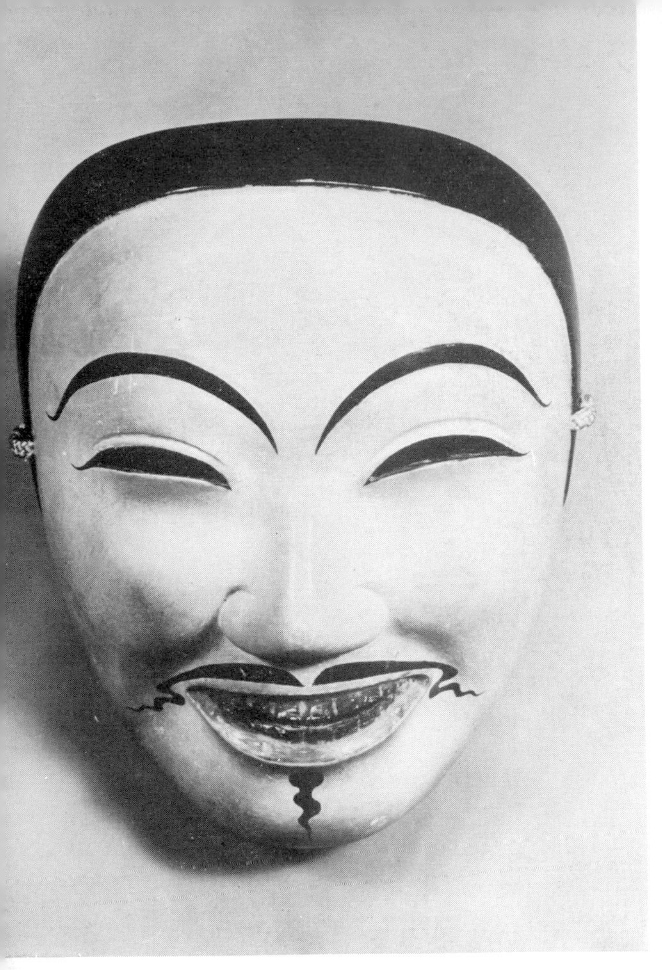

24. Bugaku mask (Right Dance): "Chikyû"

25. Bugaku mask (Right Dance): "Kitoku"

26. "Ninjô-mai" from "Sonokoma" A "Mikagura" (traditional court music) dance.

27. Wagon player

28. Wagon

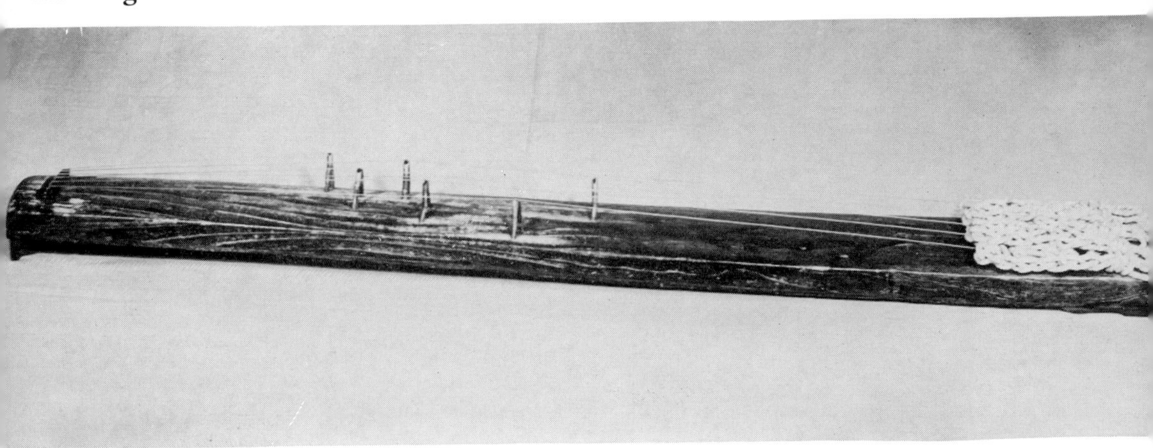

29. Noh stage

30. Noh play: "Funabenkei"

31. Noh play: "Hagorom

32. Noh-kan (Fue) player

33. Noh-kan

34. Kotsuzumi player

35. Kotsuzumi

36. Otsuzumi player

37. Otsuzun

38. Taiko player

39. Taiko

40. Hoyô (a Buddhist ceremony)

41. Sange ("Scattering Flowers." A Buddhist rite.)

42. Dôbatsu (cymbal)

43. Rei (bell)

44. Kin (gong)

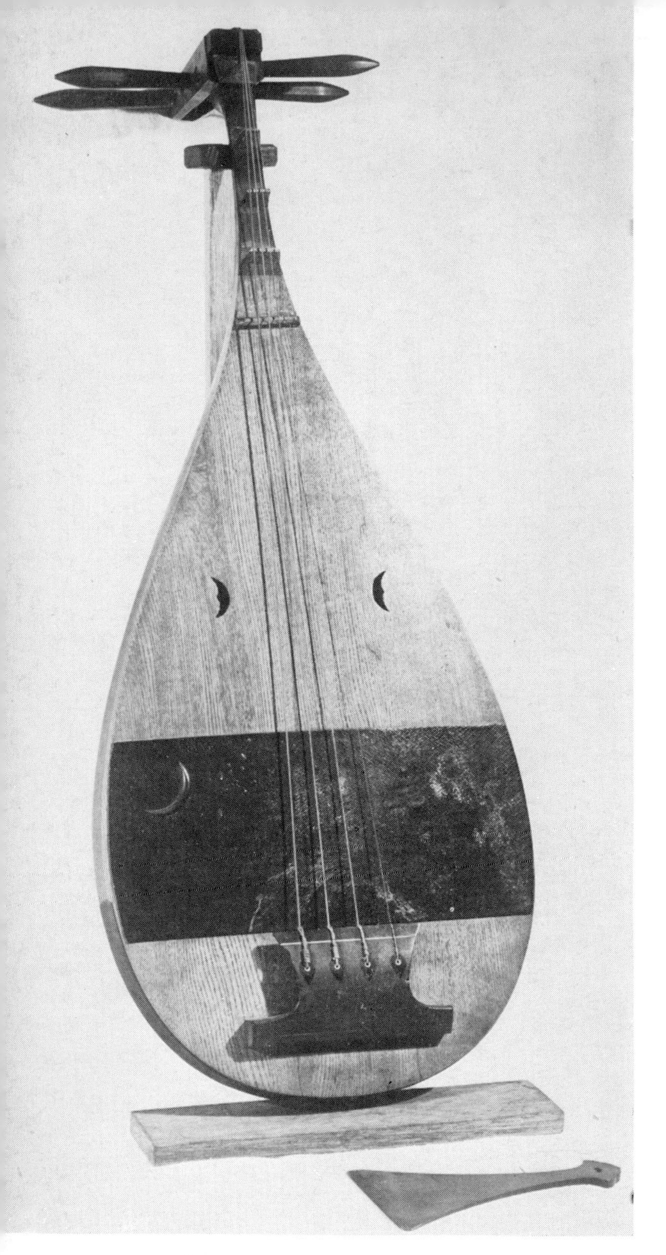

45. Heike-biwa

46. Sasabiwa (or Kôjinbiwa)

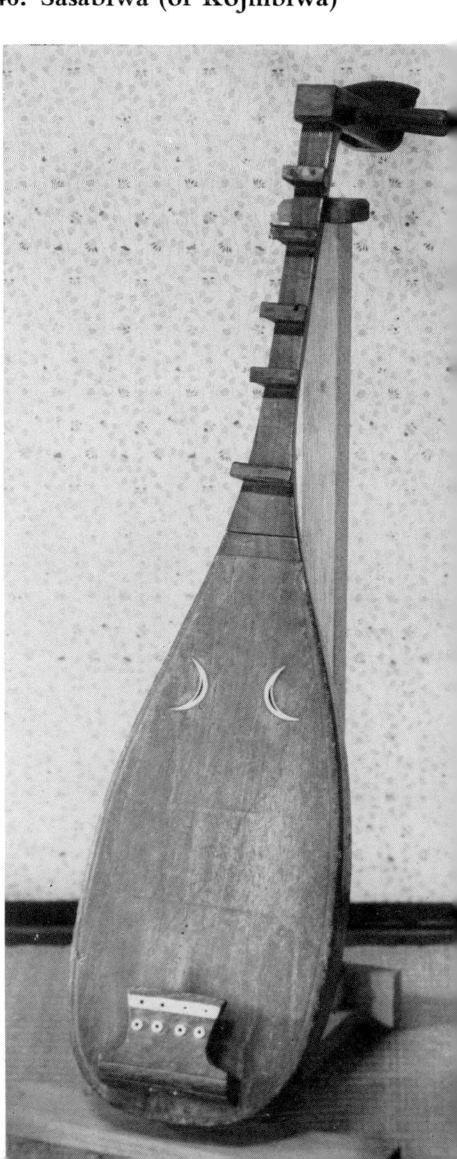

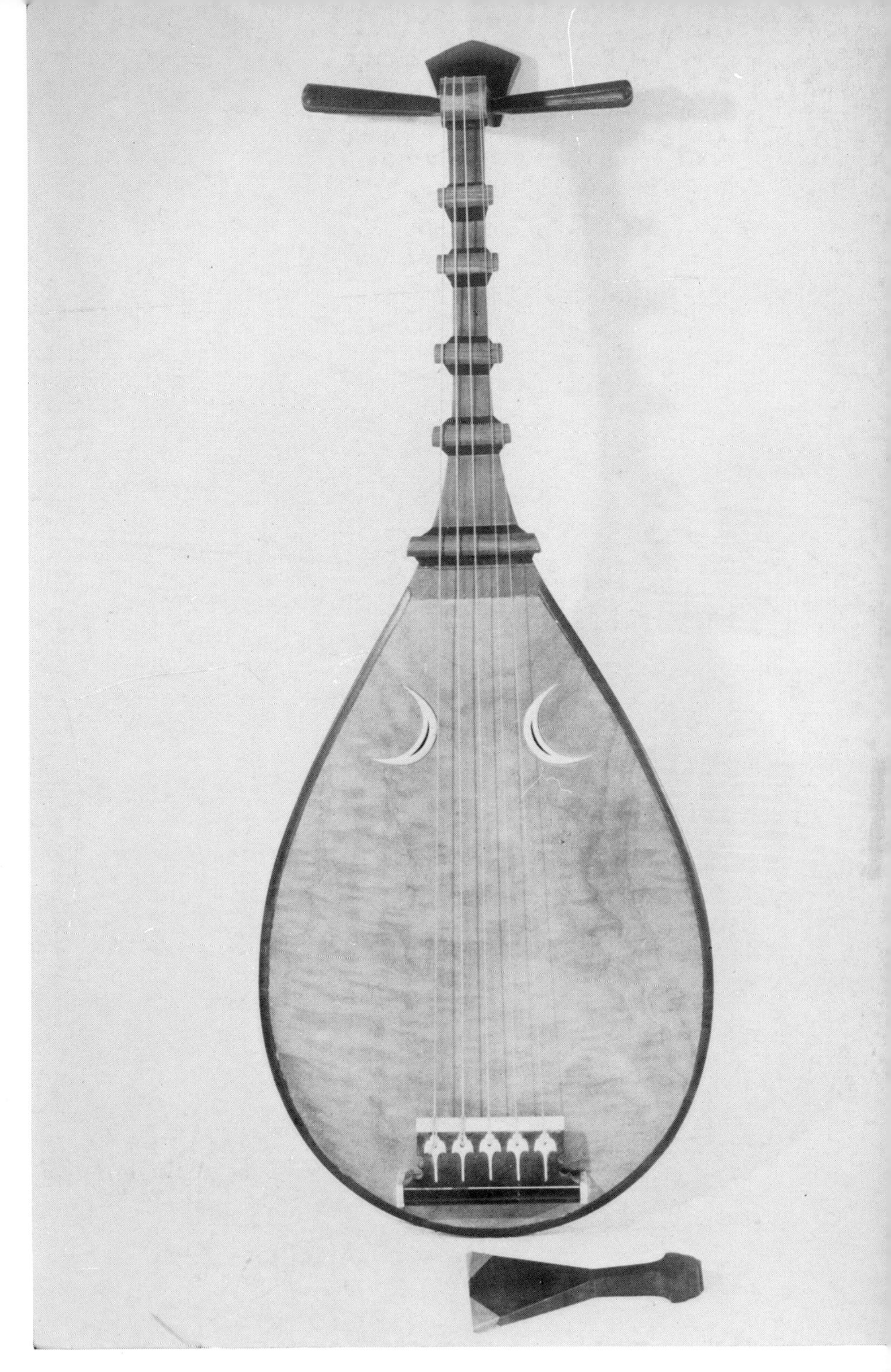

47. Chikuzenbiwa

48. Sankyoku (ensemble of Koto of the Yamada School, Shamisen, and Shakuhachi

49. Koto (Ikuta School)

50. Shakuhachi player

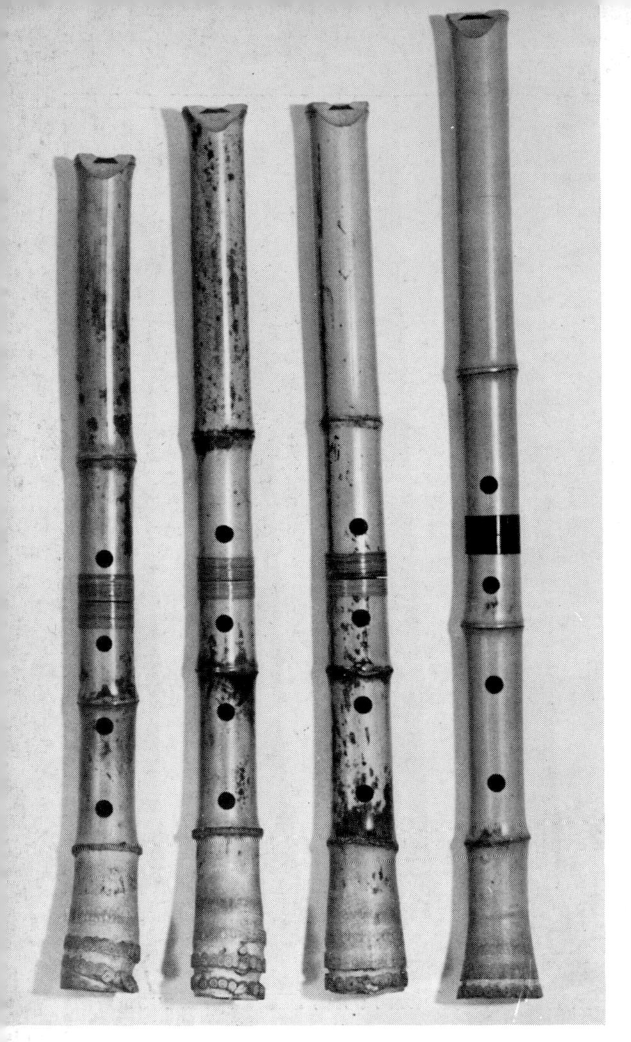

51. Sakuhachi of different pitches

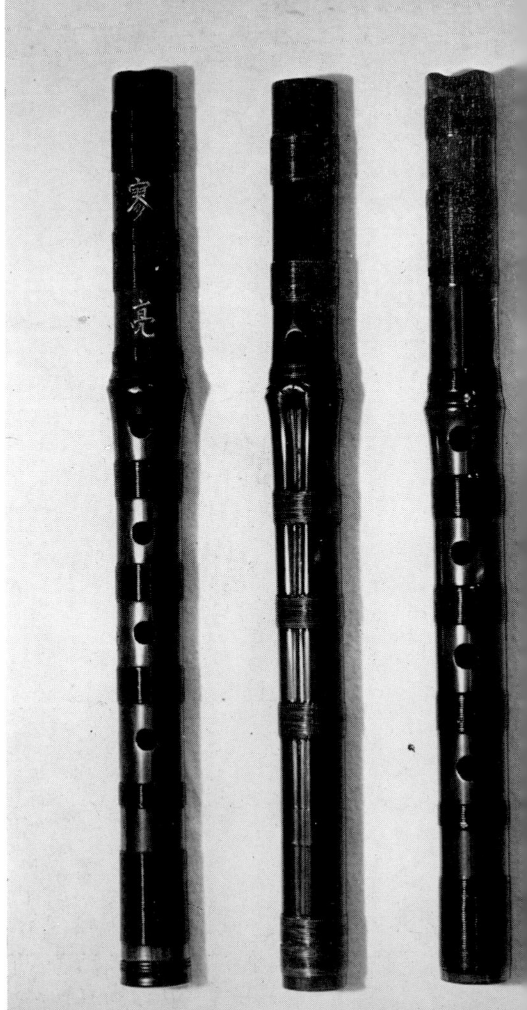

52. Hitoyogiri (the pipe in the centre shows the other side)

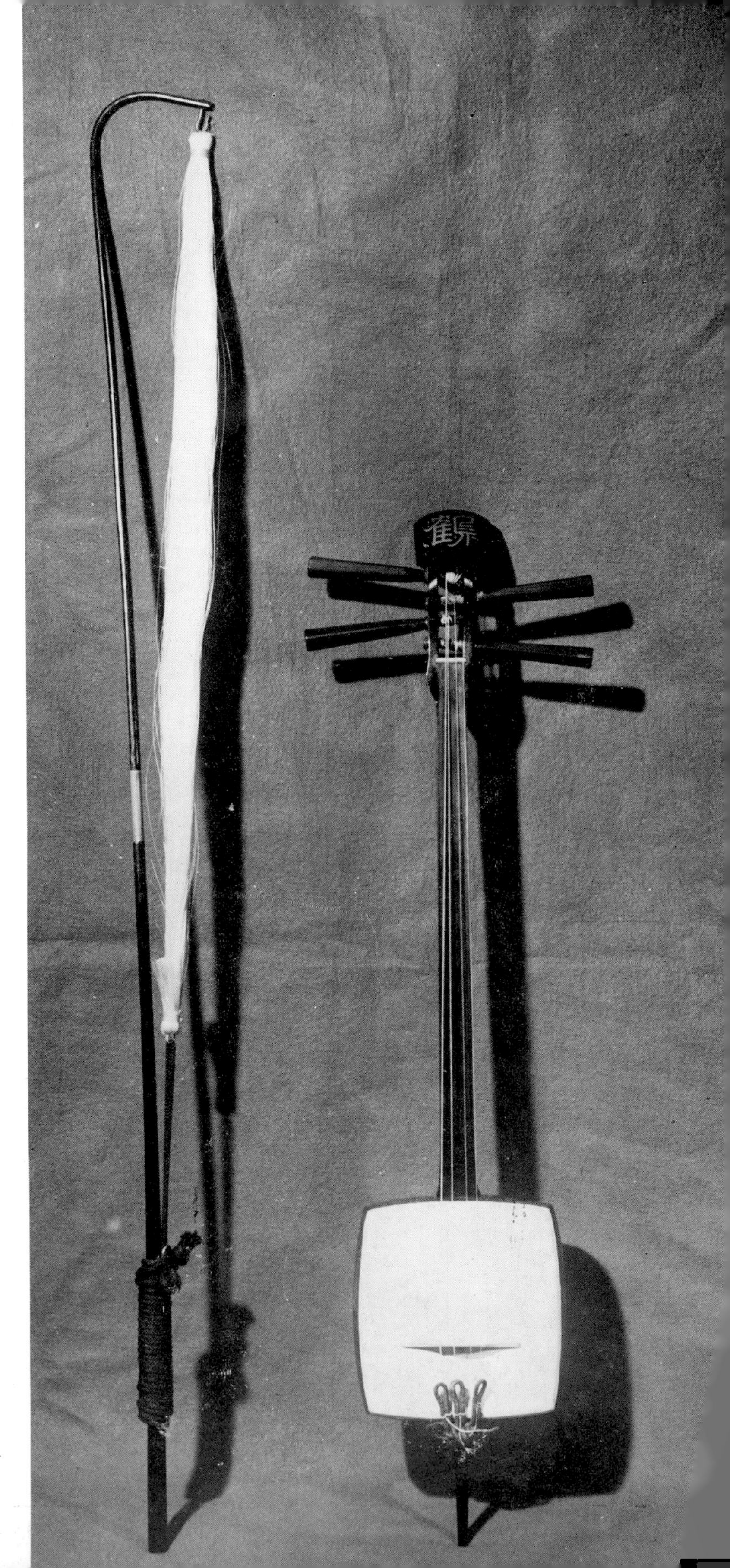

53. Kokyû

54. Kabuki dance: "Yasuna" Accompanied by four singers and three Shamisen players of Kiyomoto.

55. Kabuki dance: "Asazuma-bune" Accompanied by eight singers and eight Shamisen players of Nagauta.

56. Shamisen player of Gidayû

57. Bunraku puppet play: "Horikawa Sarumawashi no Dan"
A Gidayû singer and a Shamisen accompanist are on the right.

58. Shamisen player of Nagauta

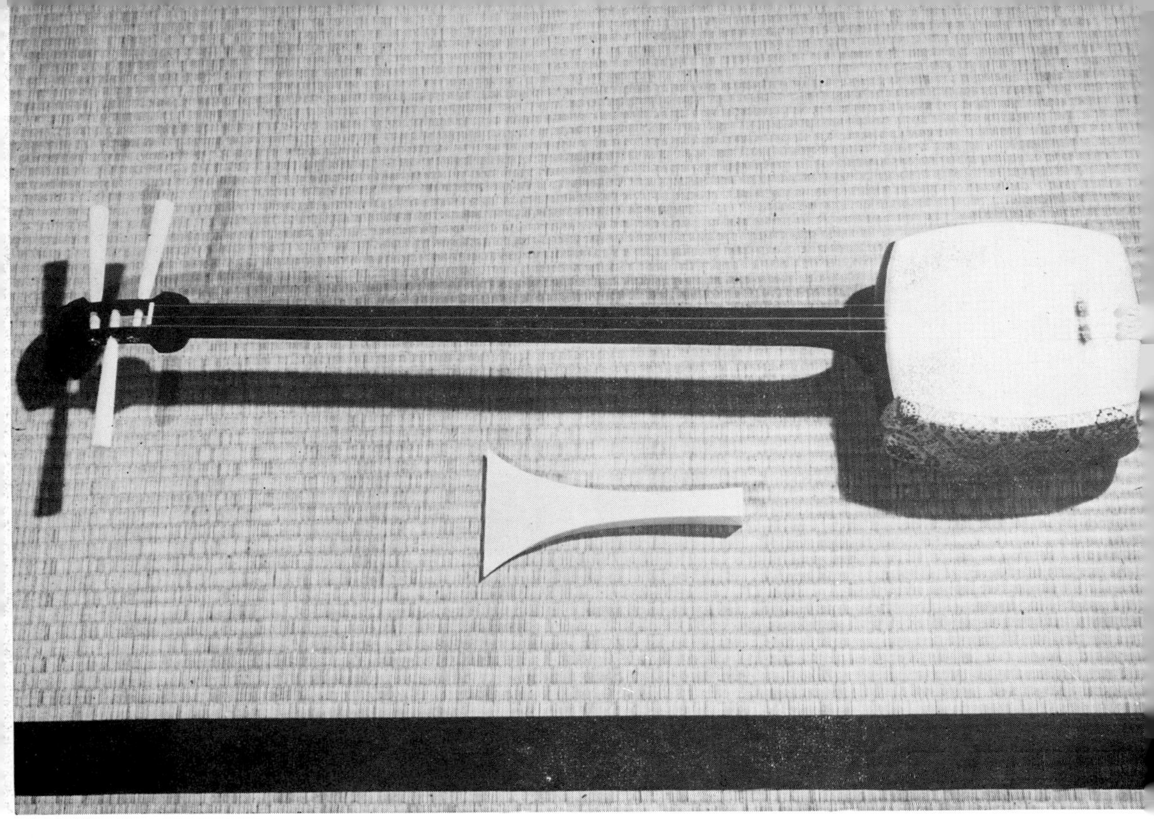

59. Nagauta Shamisen

60. Construction of the Nagauta Shamisen

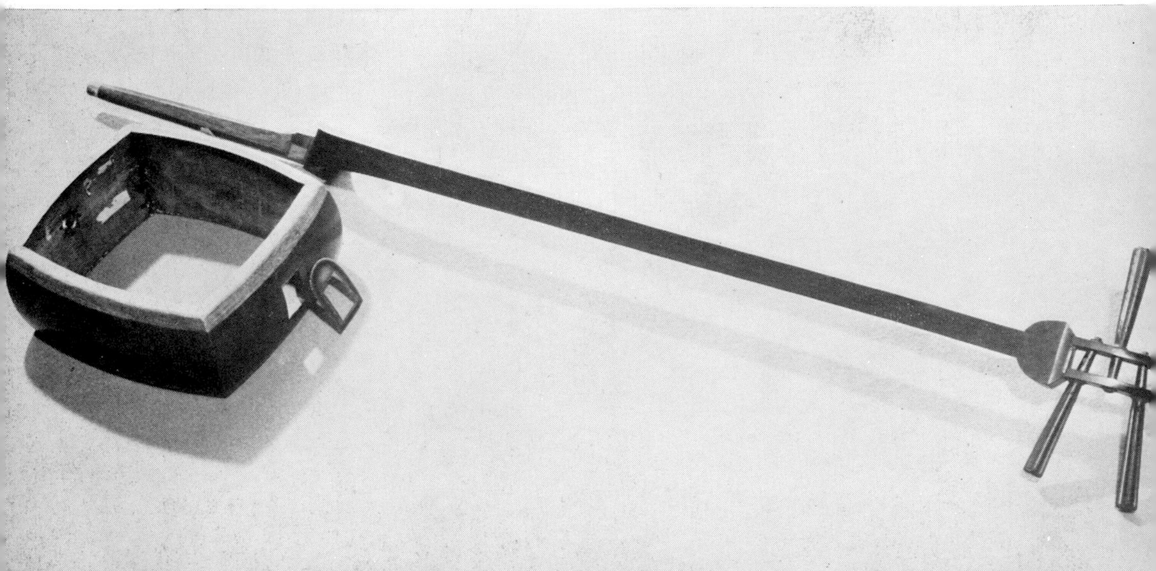

61. Kabuki stage and audience (Edo period Ukiyoe)

62. Kabuki rehearsal (Edo period Ukiyoe)

63. Atarigane, Kabuki Geza music.

64. Orugoru (Orgel). Kabuki Geza music.

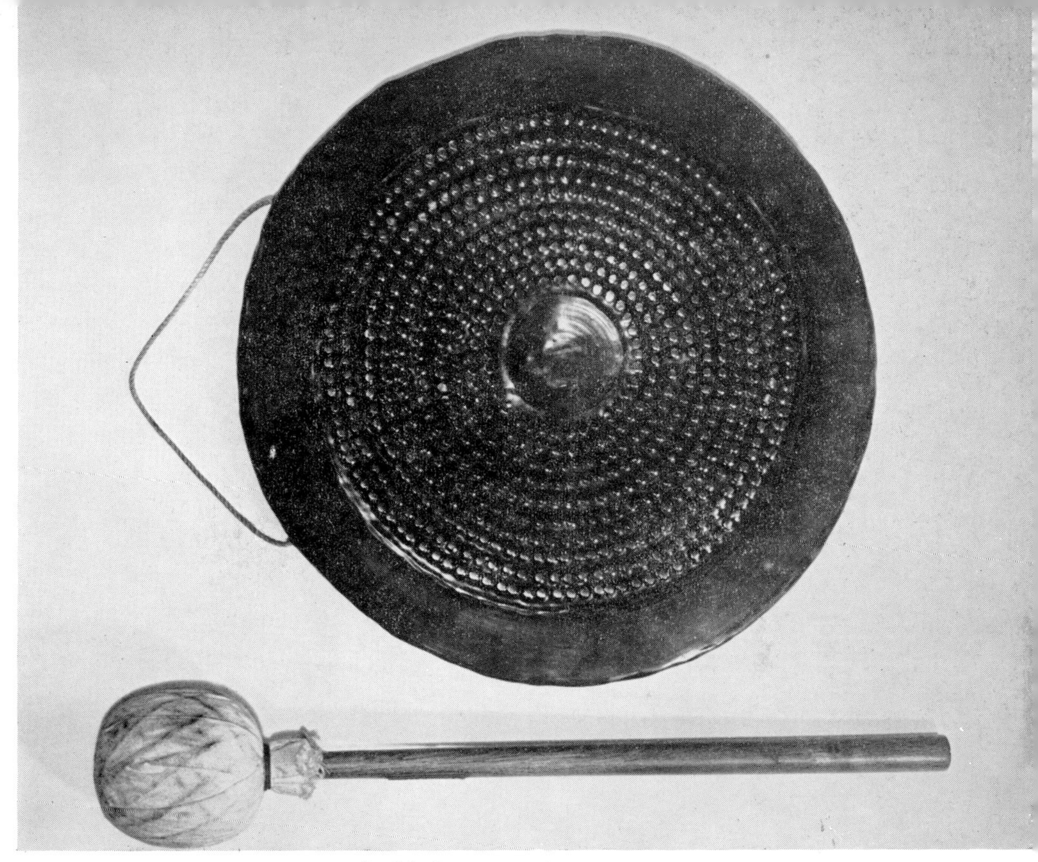

65. Dora (gong). Kabuki Geza music.

66. Chappa (cymbals). Kabuki Geza music

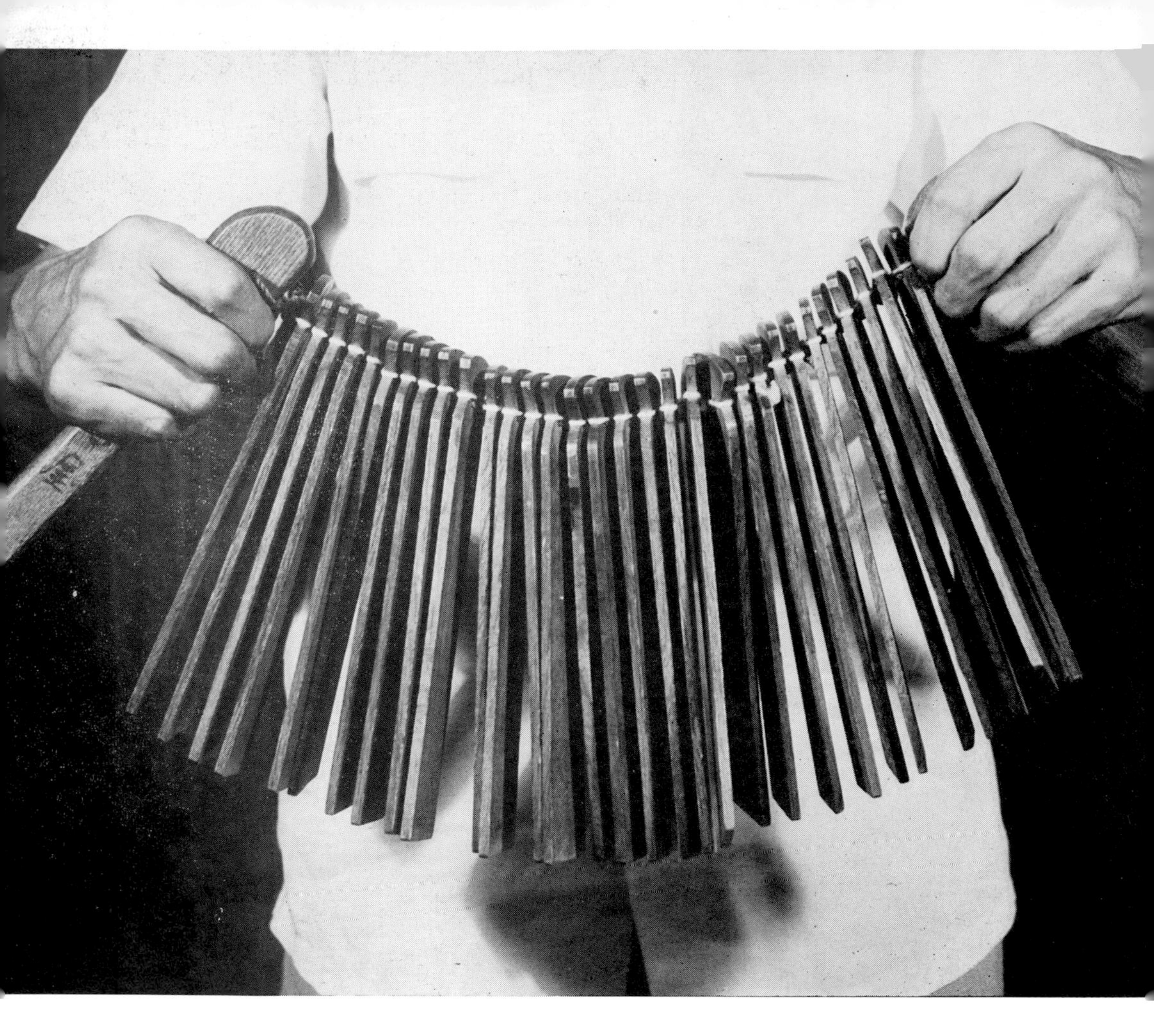

67. Binzasara (clapper). Kabuki Geza music.

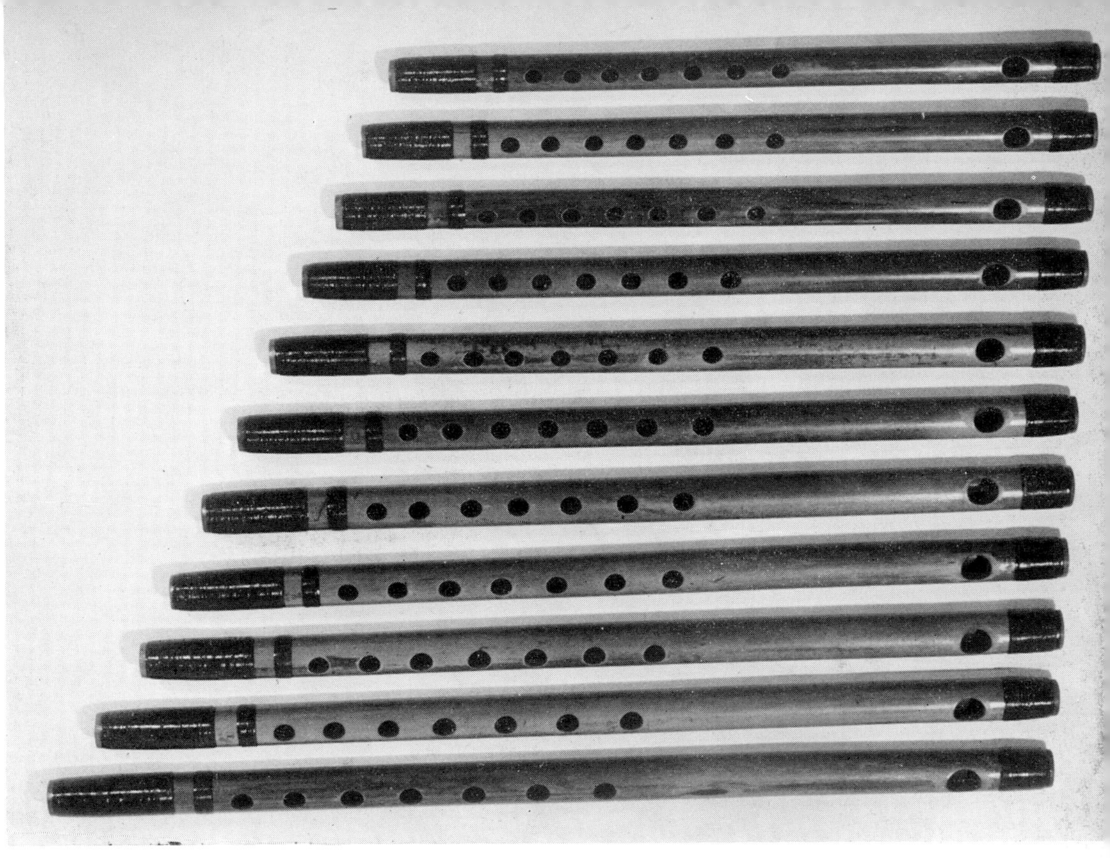

68. Shimobue, Kabuki Geza music.

69. Daibyoshi
Kabuki Geza music.

70. "Shishi Odori" Folk dance of Iwate Prefecture.

71. "Osuwa Daiko" Folk music of Nagano Prefecture with drum ensemble.

72. "Hayashida" Rice planting song and dance in Hiroshima Prefecture.

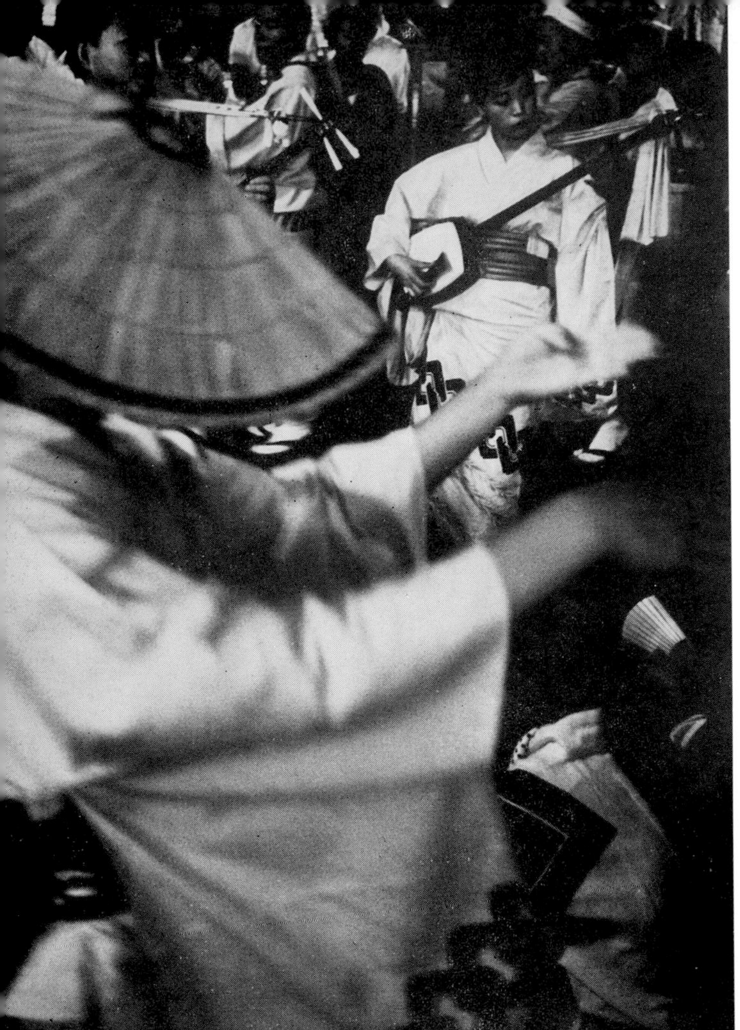

73. "Kaze no Bon"
Folk dance of Toyama Prefecture. Bon dancers stroll through streets accompanied by Shamisen players.

74. "Izumo Kagura"
Folk dance in a Shinto shrine of Shimane Prefecture.

75. "Nembutsu Odori"
Buddhist chant of the Jôdo sect in Nagano Prefecture.

76. Yamato-goto (two-stringed zither for Shinto ceremonies)

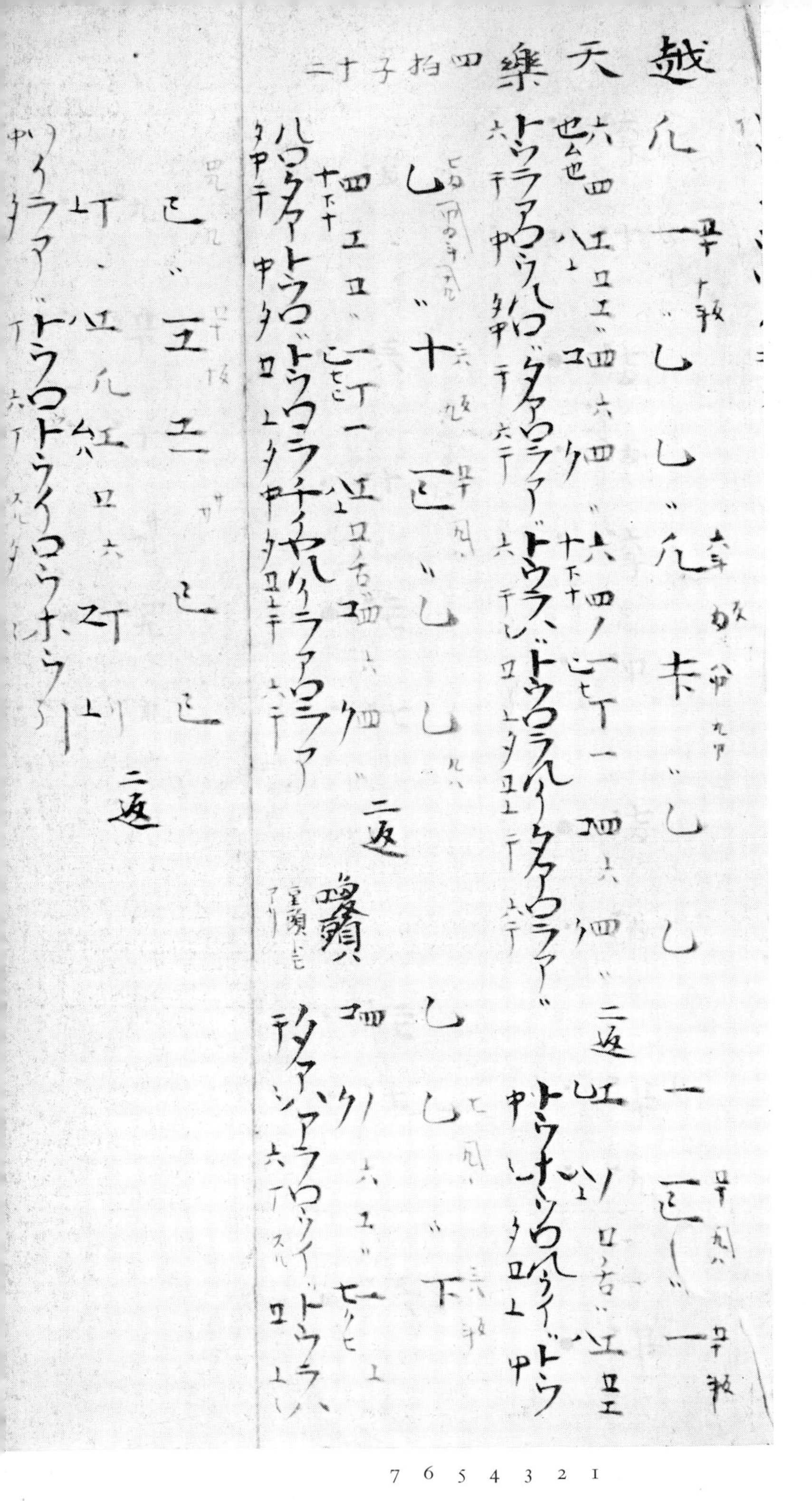

77. Kangen score (manuscript written in the beginning of the 17th century): "Etenraku
The ensemble instruments are represented by seven vertical lines respectively indicating (1) Koto, (2) Shô, (3) Koto (not discernible in the photograph due to its being written in red ink), (4) Ryût (5) Biwa, (6) Hichiriki solmization, and (7) Hichiriki fingering. The Koto appears twice due to th that different tablatures are used for this instrument depending on the method adopted by the pl

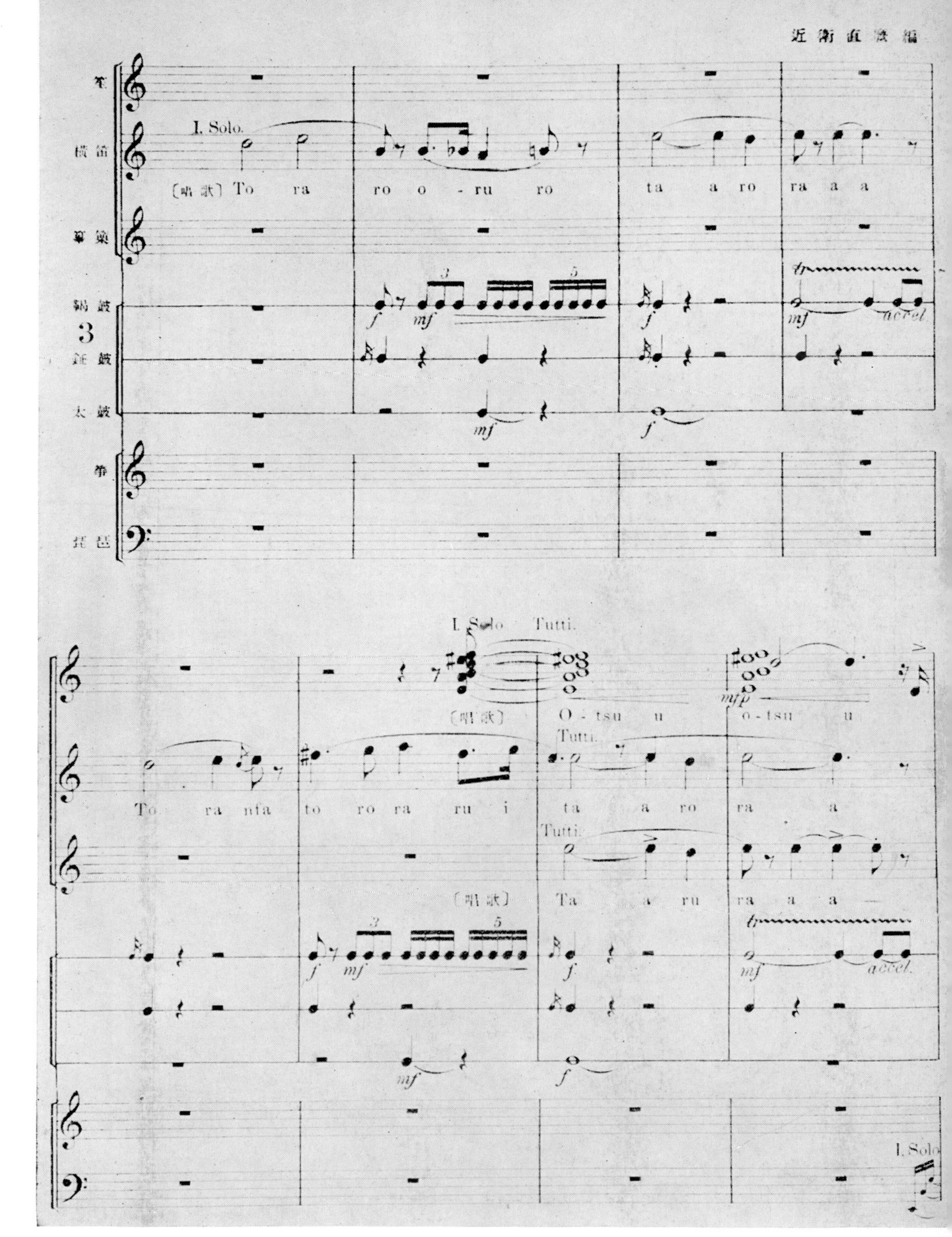

78. Kangen score: "Etenraku" A transciption of the beginning part of the score shown on the facing page. From the top, notations for Shô, Ryûteki, Hichiriki, Kakko, Shôko, Taiko, Koto, and Biwa.

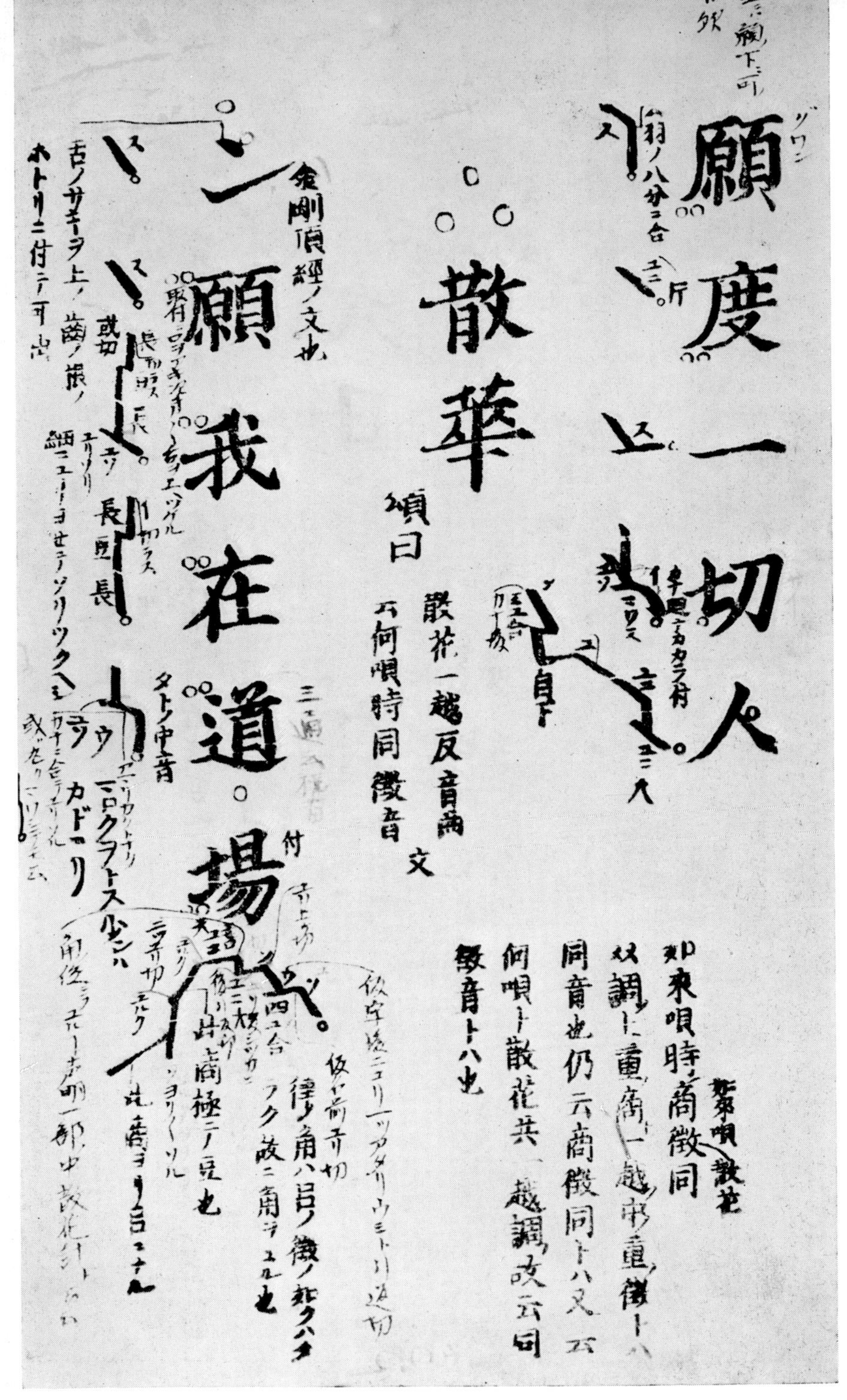

79. Shomyo (Buddhist chant) notation: "Sange" From the "Gyozan Shishô" printed in 1711.

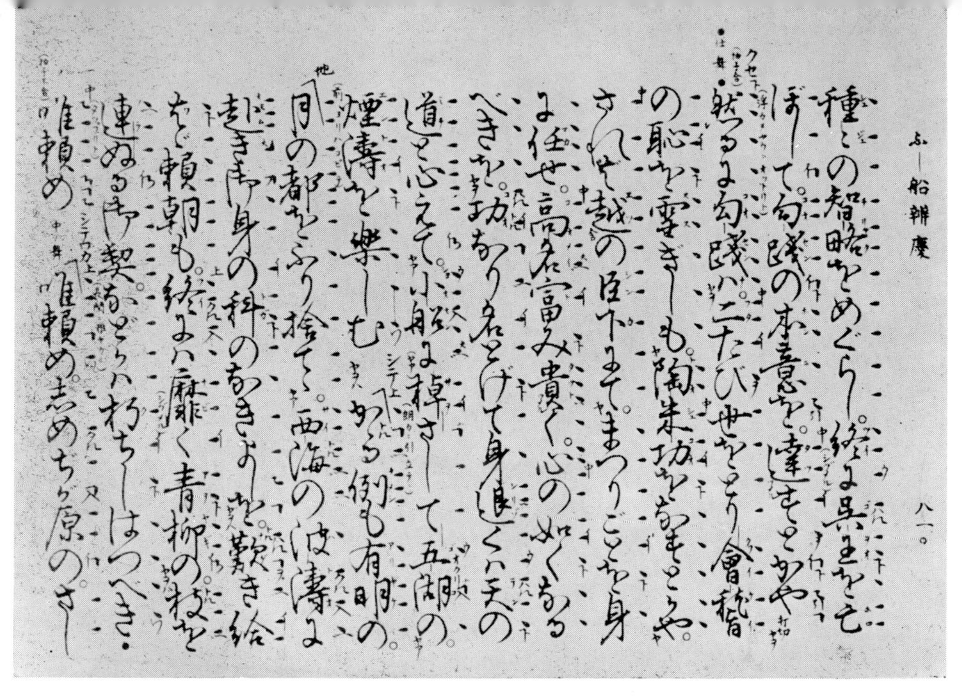

80. Text and notation for Noh chant: "Funabenkei"
The notation is marked on the right side of each line of the text.

81. Noh-kan tablature: "Banshiki Jo no Mai"

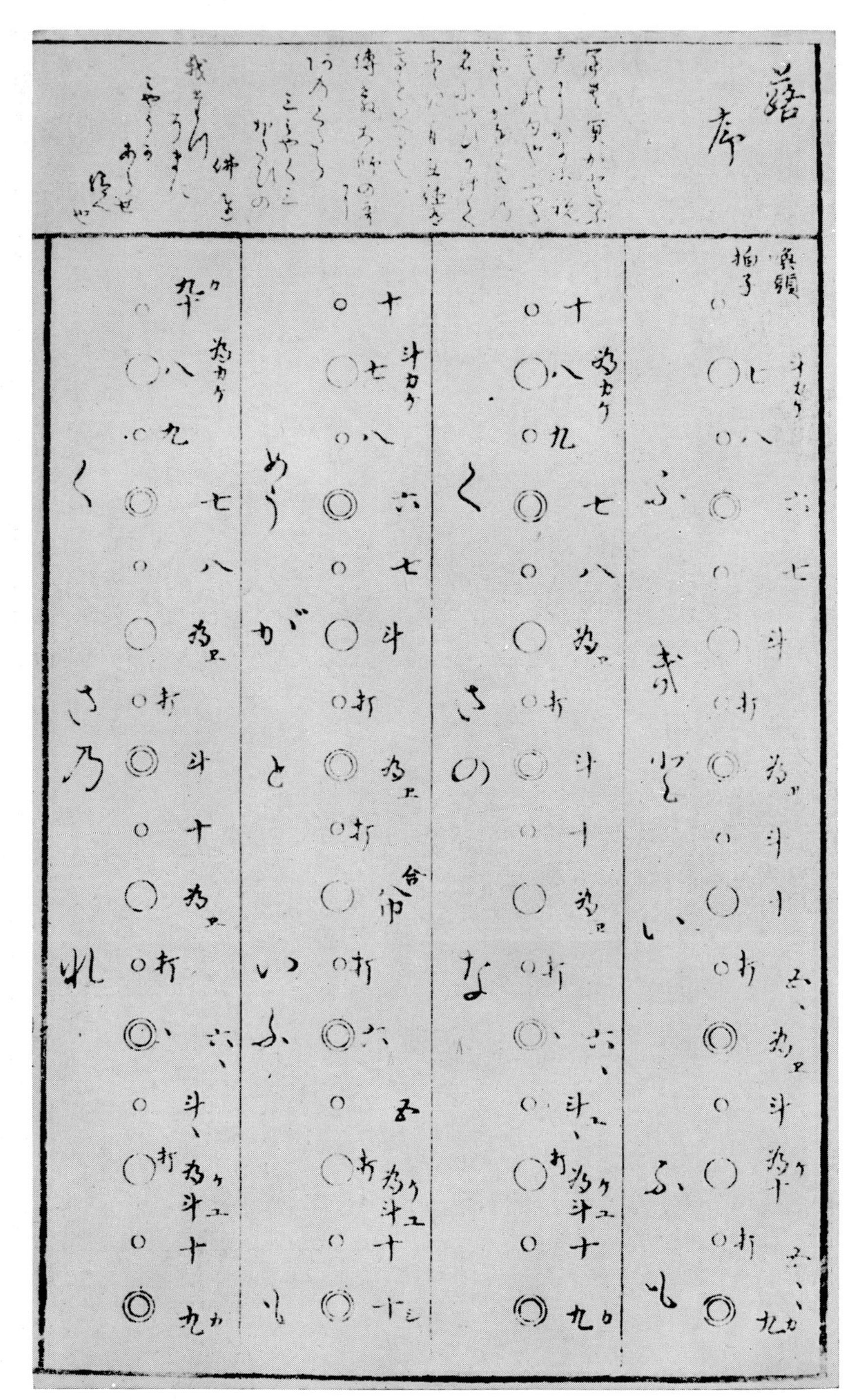

82. Koto song 'from "Sôkyoku-taiishô" printed in 1779): "Fuki" Tablature with the text in three vertical lines to a columm. The line to the right of the centre line indicates the Koto part, the centre line illustrated with circles indicates rhythm, and the line to the left of the centre line indicates the text.

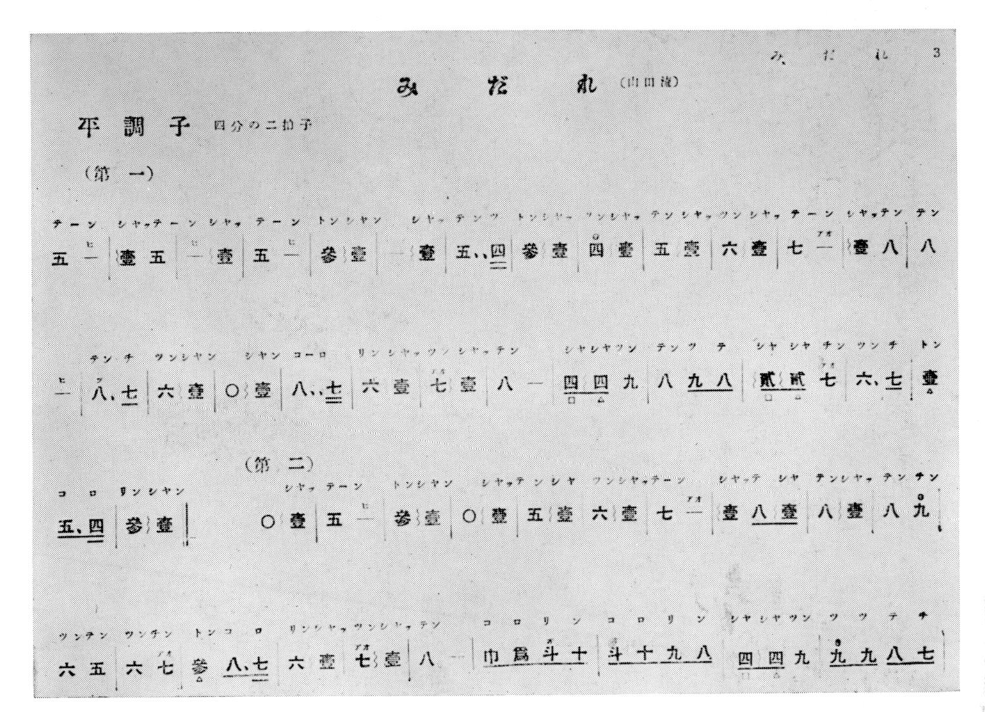

83. Koto tablature in Japanese style, now in use: "Midare"
Written horizontally and to be read from left to right. The upper lines in smaller characters indicate a kind of onomatopoeic singing of the melody, and the lower lines indicate names of strings with occasional marks for special techniques.

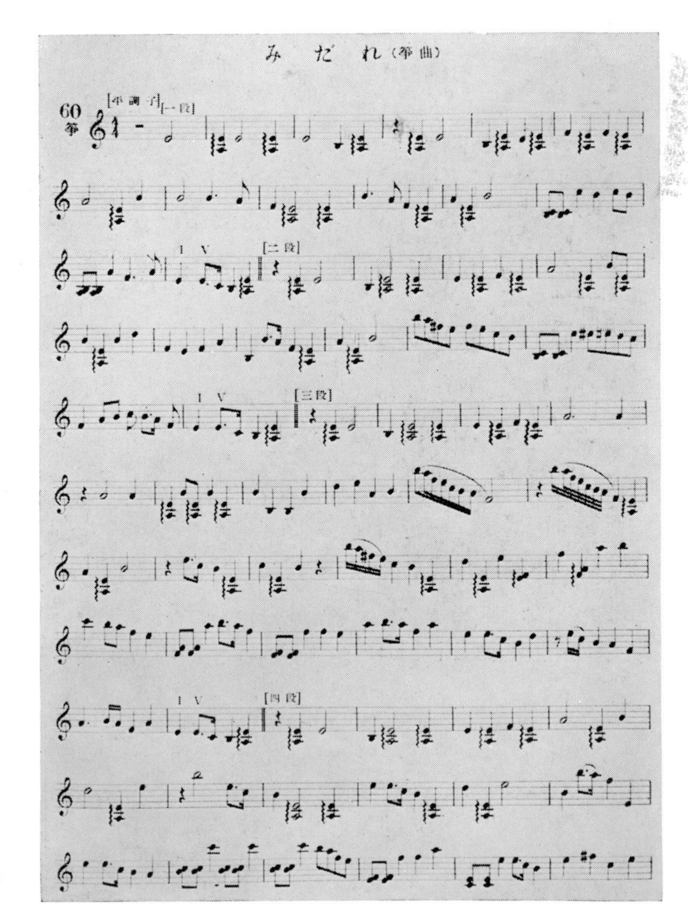

84. Transcription from the above tablature: "Midare"

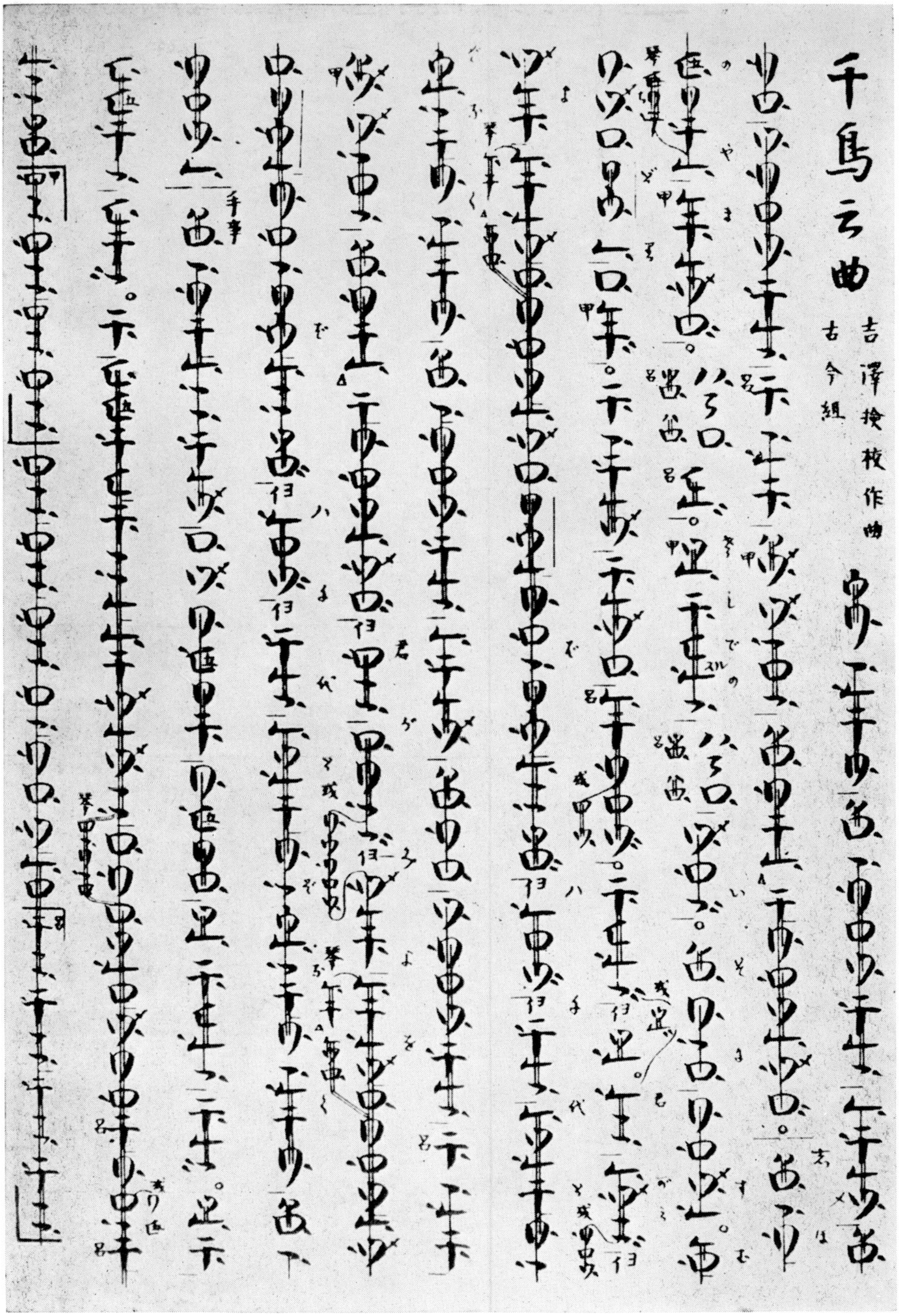

千鳥之曲

吉澤検校作曲

古今組

85. Shakuhachi tablature: "Chidori no Kyoku"

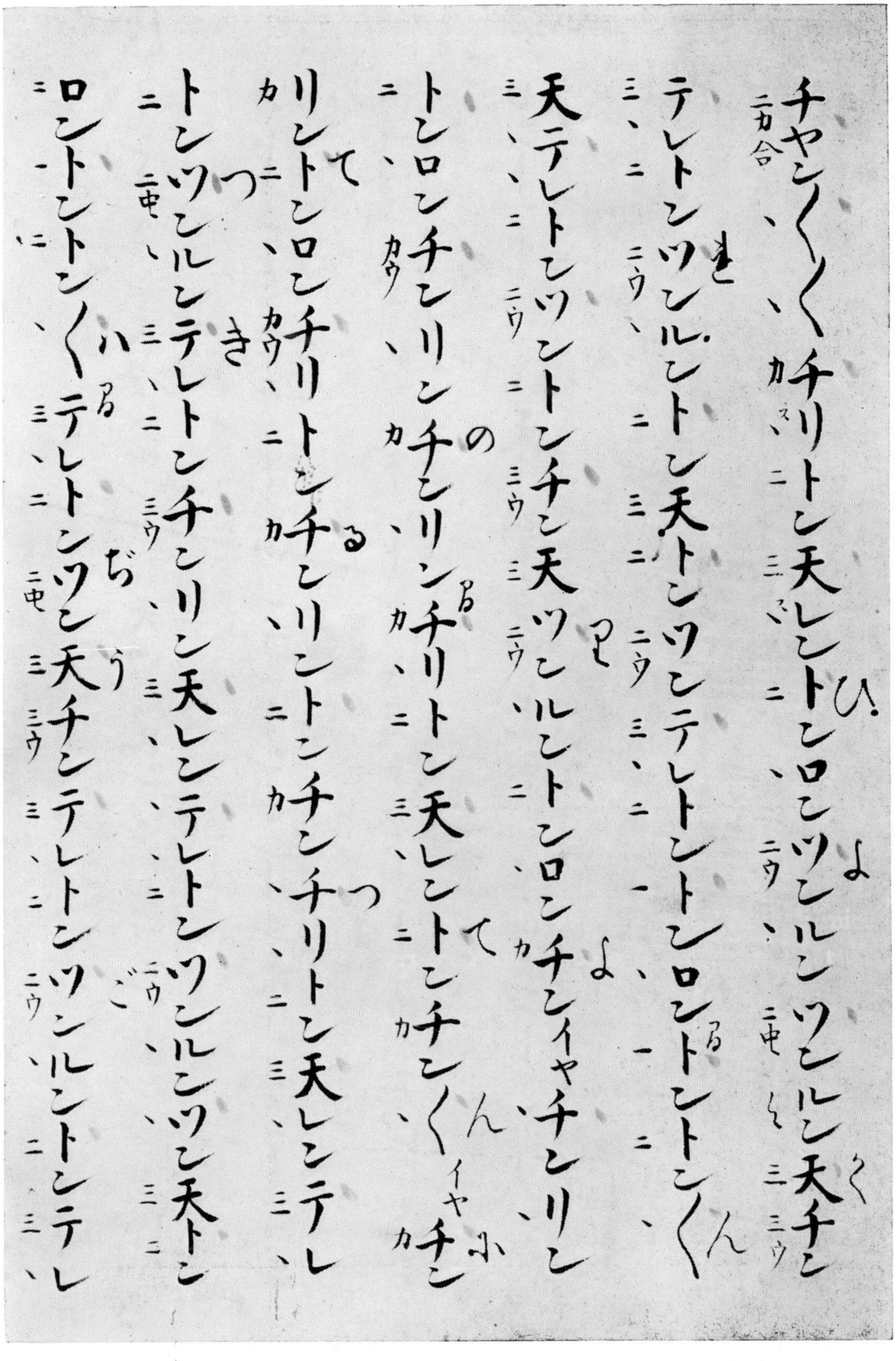

86. Shamisen Kumiuta text and tablature (manuscript written in 1769): "Ryûkyû-gumi" In groups of three vertical lines, the right-hand lines indicate the text, the centre lines indicate the onomatopoeic singing of the melody of the Shamisen, and the left-hand line indicates fingering positions on the Shamisen.

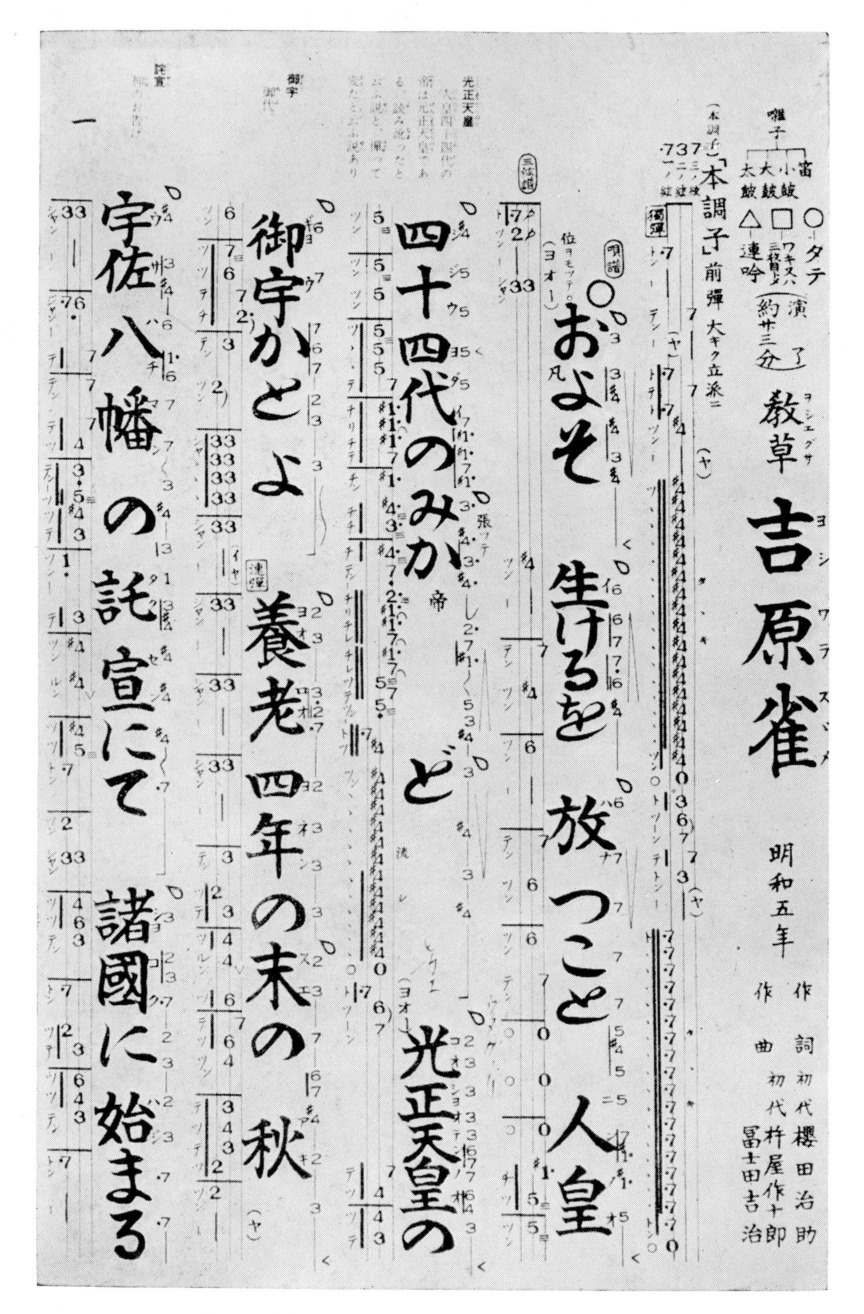

87. Present-day tablature and text of Nagauta: "Yoshiwarasuzume" Larger characters represent the text while smaller Arabic numerals to the right of the larger characters indicate the melody for chanting. Other smaller Arabic numerals on three vertical straight lines corresponding to the three strings of the Shamisen indicate the melody of Shamisen.